# PRIVATE GIVING, PUBLIC GOOD

## THE IMPACT OF PHILANTHROPY AT THE UNIVERSITY OF EDINBURGH

Jean Grier and Mary Bownes

THE UNIVERSITY
*of* EDINBURGH

Edinburgh University Press Ltd for
The University of Edinburgh
The Tun – Holyrood Road
12 (2f) Jackson's Entry
Edinburgh EH8 8PJ

www.euppublishing.com

Designed and typeset in Great Britain by
Double Dagger Book Production, and
printed and bound in Latvia by
Livonia Print

A CIP record for this book is available from the British Library

ISBN 978 0 7486 9957 5 (hardback)

# Contents

This book is dedicated to all those who have given us time, expertise or financial support – past and present – enabling the University of Edinburgh to be a world leader for 431 years

# Foreword

THE UNIVERSITY OF EDINBURGH has over 400 years of successful history educating tens of thousands of students. For many of these students financial support has been vital to enable them to attend the University. Important new academic disciplines and areas such as geology, literature, epigenetics, Bayesian statistics and regenerative medicine have been developed here. The city benefits from splendid iconic buildings such as Old College, Teviot Row Student Union and the McEwan Hall. The community benefits from public lectures, cultural events and a range of festivals including the Science Festival and the Festival Fringe. The large scale of these many and important contributions to student support, intellectual discovery, the cityscape and community engagement depends crucially on private philanthropy. Such philanthropy is not new and the University was preceded by gifts of books and property. By helping us properly understand the role of philanthropy in our life and history, Jean Grier and Mary Bownes have made a compelling contribution to the future support of the aspects of our great University that matter most. Jean and Mary have made many valuable contributions to student support, community engagement and

The Principal, Sir Timothy O'Shea

development work. This book will be their most enduring contribution and I thank them warmly for the diligent and careful work that went into its preparation.

*Professor Sir Timothy O'Shea*

### OUR CURRENT PRINCIPAL

Professor Sir Timothy O'Shea joined the University of Edinburgh in 2002 and has been a wonderful leader and ambassador for the University. Over the last twelve years the University has gone from strength to strength, rising in the world rankings, growing our numbers of staff and students from across the globe, increasing our income for research, and enabling the development of a number of spin-off companies which build on that research. He was responsible for launching the biggest and broadest fundraising campaign in the history of the University, one of the largest in the UK, and ensuring it was successfully delivered. Sir Timothy is extremely keen on widening access to the University and has actively supported this by ensuring bursaries and scholarships are a key part of our fundraising activity. With a background in computer science, information technology, artificial intelligence and especially new teaching methods, he has led us to take the risk of engaging with Massive Open Online Courses (MOOCs). These have been highly successful and have led to another 900,000 online learners interacting with the University to date. Sir Timothy is an ardent historian of the University and is a great storyteller, engaging visitors with anecdotes about how things have changed over the years, and about our buildings, collections and research expertise past and present. He is a great philanthropist in his own right having personally supported bursaries and specific projects as well as devoting huge amounts of time to fundraising on behalf of the University.

*Mary Bownes*

# Introduction

AN INSTITUTION OF THE AGE and prestige of the University of Edinburgh has much to thank its donors for over the years. The University was founded in 1583 – at that time as 'the Tounis College' (town's college), indicating its independence from both the Church and the State. From its earliest days, the University benefited from the generosity of benefactors of many types – those who gave money, those who commissioned work or sponsored a particular development, those who gave support in kind, those who gifted books, paintings and instruments and those who encouraged corporate sponsorship. This book aims to show the value of donors past and present, and to examine the difference their giving has made to the institution, to the broader community and, in many cases, to the world.

## A NOTE ON TERMINOLOGY

The University of Edinburgh did not formally adopt that title until 1685, but for the sake of brevity, this book generally uses the designation 'University' throughout.

## A NOTE ON HISTORICAL MONETARY VALUES

It is notoriously difficult to equate a past monetary value to its current equivalent. As an example, William McEwan gave £115,000 in

1886 towards the cost of the McEwan Hall. Depending on whether one uses a measure of average wages, the Retail Prices Index or some other calculation, that donation equates to anything from £883,000 to £4,430,000 in today's money. But were we to set out today to build the hall from scratch, the money would be woefully inadequate – even at the top end of that calculation – to recreate the magnificent building that is the McEwan Hall. For this reason, when figures are given in this book, no attempt has been made to specify a modern-day equivalent. Suffice it to say that Mr McEwan's donation was a very generous one, and that, for example, the £10,000 raised by the students through their 'Fancy Fair' in the same year towards the building of the Teviot Union was also a very impressive achievement.

# 1

## Benefiting from Philanthropy

A N EXAMINATION OF HOW the University has benefited from the generosity of donors could seek to catalogue gifts of all kinds over the years, and such records do exist. As a matter of course, it seems, all significant gifts and bequests were recorded in the minutes of the Senatus Academicus (which began in 1733) and later in those of University Court (established 1858, taking over governance in 1889). Until comparatively recently, gifts and bequests were also published in the University Calendar. Such records are invaluable, but it is also important to look at how the University has used donations and at how that generosity has translated into tangible benefits. These benefits may be to the University itself or, through the activities of staff and students, to society more widely. The chapters which follow are not an exhaustive record of philanthropic giving, but instead focus on some interesting case studies under a number of themes. There is much more information available elsewhere on many of the cases illustrated, and the Bibliography gives some suggestions for further reading and investigation.

Patterns of giving show, not surprisingly, a major interest by donors in funding research into medicine and veterinary medicine in particular. In some cases, this stems from a desire to recognise the excellent support an individual or family has had from the relevant profession when facing a particular illness. In other cases, a more general wish to contribute to advances in the sciences is evident. An interest in a particular geographic region – whether from living there or simply visiting – may lead to donations for research with a regional focus. The University has also benefited from gifts of objects including books and manuscripts, musical instruments, geological specimens, works of art and many other items. Some of these objects have an intrinsic value, and all the collections to which these items have been added provide a valuable teaching and research resource.

As indicators of the extent of philanthropy over the years, a review of bequests and endowments to the then Faculty of Medicine in 1986 revealed that there were over 280 funds in existence. Some of these were quite narrow in scope, making them difficult to use in the modern day, and for that reason, the most beneficial way of providing funding to the University is to minimise restrictions. Funds earmarked for research into smallpox or polio, for example, are thankfully no longer needed for that purpose; similar 'redundancies' may hopefully be possible for HIV/AIDS research in the future, and longer term for other illnesses too, though new diseases will emerge and need support.

Many donations carry with them a responsibility on the part of the University to facilitate their support over many years into the future; the generous bequest by William McEwan in the nineteenth century which enabled the building of the McEwan Hall has ironically left the University with a major task to face in the twenty-first century, as the hall needs significant investment to cover its maintenance and essential repairs, and to allow for the refurbishment and repurposing of this building of international importance. The University of Edinburgh has a very high proportion of fine listed buildings. Whilst valuing our built heritage, listing brings restrictions on how these buildings can be altered and used, and on how access legislation and reduced energy consumption expectations can be met, as well as increasing the costs of their routine maintenance.

Robert Barker's panorama of Edinburgh from Calton Hill

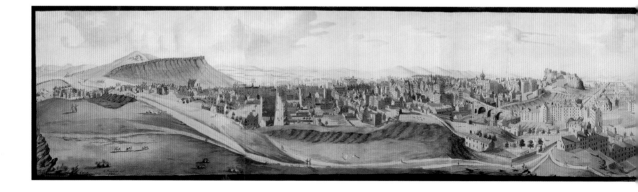

Some of the earliest benefactions to the University were very practical. Clement Litill's bequest of his library predated the founding of the University and is now commemorated in a mesostic poem carved into the pavement outside the Main Library in George Square. Inclusion of the poem in the pavement was just one part of a major redevelopment which began in 2009 at a cost of over £60 million; the redevelopment has turned the Main Library into a state-of-the-art modern space used intensively by students. One hundred years after the establishment of the University, in around 1689–93, Sir John Foulis of Ravelston paid between £20 and £30 per annum for his son's education, when the official fee level was just £2 for Edinburgh residents. Opinions seem to be divided on whether this was a voluntary overpayment – effectively a donation to support others in an ethos of the rich supporting the less well-off – or whether an element of means-testing was at work.

Other donors have sponsored research, either directly or through the foundation of chairs or other posts. These are key, as they allow the development of new areas and new directions of scholarship. When the University was founded, the range of academic disciplines covered was very limited; but we have long had a mixture of the professions, such as law and medicine, coupled with basic research and scholarship and the ethos to use these to make a real difference to people's lives around the world.

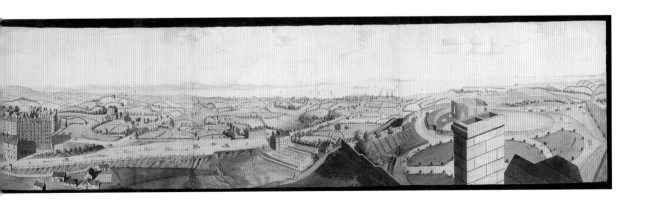

In this fresco, painted around 1510
in the Apostolic Palace in Vatican
City, Raphael imagines the School
of Athens, arguably the world's
first university. Plato is conversing
with his contemporary, Aristotle,
surrounded by Greek philosophers
from other periods

# 2

## Our Heritage

N O UNIVERSITY IS CREATED in isolation, and this chapter sets the establishment of the University of Edinburgh in the national historical context, whilst also looking at what was happening across Europe.

### THE HISTORICAL CONTEXT:
### SCOTLAND IN THE SIXTEENTH CENTURY

Founded in 1583, the University of Edinburgh (though not under that name initially) came into being at a time of great political, religious and social upheaval, not just in Scotland but across Europe. For centuries, Scotland's fortunes had been dominated by either war or open hostility with England. The Auld Alliance, a treaty first concluded between Scots and French rulers at the end of the thirteenth century and renewed in every reign thereafter, pledged France's support for Scotland's independence. Scotland's chief trading links lay with France, the Baltic and the Netherlands. As a result, very few Scots went to the universities of Oxford or Cambridge. In the fourteenth century, most went to Italy or France. By the fifteenth century, the majority of ambitious would-be scholars went to universities in the Low Countries – and especially Louvain – or to Paris.

In turn, it would largely be Scots scholars trained at Paris or Louvain who staffed the new Scottish universities – the three colleges at St Andrews, founded between 1412 and 1538; Glasgow, founded in 1451; and Aberdeen, first established in 1495. Each of these had been

By the 1580s, Louvain was a compact and well-developed city, with an established university

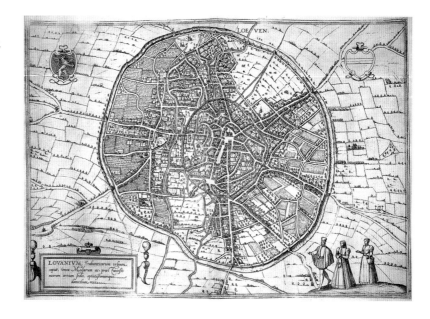

A German woodcut from the sixteenth century showing the burning of books at the gates of Wittenberg, part of the move away from the Latin of the Catholic Church

founded by a bishop and was based on a papal decree. The basic purpose of the universities was the training of the clergy of the Catholic Church. The language of instruction was Latin, as it was in the feeder grammar schools which were mostly located in burghs. Yet, steadily, the needs of society were changing. The growth of the State inevitably fed a demand for more lawyers. All 'learned in the law' were themselves clerics but the sixteenth century also saw the growth of the figure of the lay notary, men who advised on private legal matters without being members of the clergy.

The Protestant Reformation of 1560, an invasion by an English army to give support to the self-styled Lords of the Congregation opposed to the marriage of Mary, Queen of Scots to the Dauphin of France, brought an end to the Auld Alliance and marked the establishment of a novel relationship with England – the 'amity', a word that had a distinctly Protestant ring to it. The new alliance, based on a mutual religion, brought a new political and religious dynamic. The troubled Scottish borderland began to experience an unwonted stability. Scotland's new Protestant religion, now a culture of the vernacular rather than of the Latin of the Catholic Church, relied heavily on English prayer books, catechisms and bibles, especially the Geneva Bible compiled by English religious exiles in Geneva in the late 1550s.

In other respects, however, relations with England changed little. Scots did not suddenly flood into English universities after 1560; that did not happen much before the eighteenth century. Despite a predominantly Catholic France and the ongoing religious strife between Catholics and Protestants in the Netherlands, the majority of Scots continued to go to those countries to study. They went to the same universities in France and the Netherlands as before 1560, especially to gain a specialist second degree, either in theology or law, although they also started to frequent the new Huguenot *académies* such as Montauban and Saumur from the 1570s onwards. Law itself remained rooted in canon (church) law, both before and after the Reformation. And although Protestantism, in both Scotland and England, was a religion of the vernacular, Latin firmly remained the language of scholarship.

This German illustration from 1538 satirises the corruptions of the Catholic Church in Germany, where the Protestant Reformation happened earlier than in Scotland

In other kinds of foreign or overseas links, continuity was more evident than change. Trade routes remained much along the same lines as before, concentrated on the Baltic, Netherlands and France. Overland or coastal trade with England did not increase much until the very last decades of the seventeenth century. Where new markets opened up, such as grain and timber imports from Scandinavia, they involved foreign rather than English ports. And in England itself, although there were established communities of foreign merchants in ports such as Norwich and Hull as well as in London, the Scots did not establish anything like such a permanent presence. One reason lay with the nervousness of the English authorities, who disliked the prospect of foreigners with a nominally common language but a decidedly different strain of Calvinism.

The new Protestant reformers in Scotland, as in England, remained watchful of hostile foreign powers and fearful of an international Catholic conspiracy against a fledgling Protestant Church and State. In Scotland, they pinned many of their hopes on a godly monarch, the infant James VI, son of Mary, Queen of Scots (1542–67). Mary was deposed and James (1567–1625) was crowned in 1567. The 1580s, the decade which saw the birth of Edinburgh's university, was also the period when the young king began to take on the reins of power, amidst continuing fears of Catholic intrigue or invasion.

James VI of Scotland (James I of England) by Cornelius Jansens

Mary, Queen of Scots, by an unknown artist

UNIVERSITIES IN EUROPE, FROM FOUNDATION
TO THE SIXTEENTH CENTURY

The university in Europe has a long – if broken – history, originating with Plato's 'Academy', which was founded in Athens in around 387 BC. Although the academy, in various forms, lasted for 900 years, little is known about it. The focus of teaching was probably mathematics and philosophy, and perhaps civil service skills and astronomy. It may have borne greater resemblance to a debating society where members posed questions to be solved by others, and probably lacked a formal structure of teachers and students. It was not open to the public, but did not charge fees, and is known to have accepted at least two women into its ranks. It bore little resemblance to the universities of today, but nevertheless it laid the foundations for later universities. The Platonic Academy was closed down by Emperor Justinian in AD 529.

Mosaic from Pompeii depicting Plato and his pupils, second century

Unwittingly, the same Justinian also indirectly caused the birth of the first university at Bologna. Disputes over the contradictory legal frameworks in the Eastern Roman Empire caused Justinian to order an authoritative compilation of laws, the *Corpus Iuris Civilis*, including the *Digest*. Alongside so many other things, these laws fell out of favour and were forgotten during the 'Dark Ages', when monasteries and cathedral schools were among the very few places to preserve knowledge through the Early Middle Ages. Figures such as Alcuin of York and Charlemagne promoted the creation of monastic schools to preserve and teach the old Latin and Greek texts. A turning point came when the *Digest* was rediscovered in Italy in 1070, around the start of the High Middle Ages. Scholars flocked to Bologna, home to educated churchmen, in order to study the *Digest*. Many scholars came from abroad, and were subject to city laws that punished all foreigners for the crimes of any one of their fellow countrymen. Objecting to this treatment, and as students of the law, they set up mutual help organisations along national lines to combat these laws, operating much like medieval guilds but for groups of foreign students. These groups – *nationes* – would then pay for professors to teach them. Over time, the *nationes* came together and eventually formed a collective, encompassing all: a *universitas*.

This again operated more like a guild of students than as a body of central leadership, although with time its powers grew to regulate the pay and employment of professors, course material and duration of study. Until the *universitas* took control of these functions, the professors had operated entirely freelance. Similar systems of freelance professors and corporations of students existed in Paris,

Oxford and Salamanca in the eleventh and twelfth centuries. While students came to these towns primarily to learn law, as in Bologna, these places had a collection of monastic or ecclesiastic schools and associated scholars, the legal and ecclesiastic worlds being closely intertwined at the time. The monastic influence at the university in Paris was very clear – students wore tonsures and gowns, and were subject to Church law, not the king's law. Meanwhile, in England, monastic orders, bishops or wealthy individuals would often arrange dormitories and associations for students; these groupings took over from the *nationes* and became the colleges as at Oxford, Cambridge and elsewhere, granting them a greater degree of freedom from the Church than other universities. Teaching remained firmly centred on law and theology across Europe, but important structural developments arose on the continent. The corporation or guild of students at Paris came to include both teachers and students, paving the way for the modern university, while at Salamanca a formal royal charter and monetary endowment was established – as well as the first use of the word 'university' in the title of the institution.

Disputes over academic freedom and legal freedom caused the creation or expansion of many of the early universities: Oxford was greatly enlarged after foreign students were banned from Paris. In turn, legal disputes in Oxford – and a mass brawl – led to students and teachers setting up in Cambridge. Similarly, universities at Padua and Siena were formed and expanded by students leaving Bologna. The papacy was another important source for the creation of early universities, with the Pope issuing charters or 'papal bulls' to create new universities (St Andrews, Scotland; La Sapienza, Rome) or to unite ecclesiastic schools (Montpellier, France). Papal approval was also sought by those seeking to create universities (Coimbra, Portugal; Uppsala, Sweden). When Count Raymond VII was accused of supporting heretics in 1229, the King of France and the Pope commanded Raymond to create the University of Toulouse as atonement. Papal bulls continued to establish universities throughout Europe for several centuries, and from the early 1500s did so eagerly in the Spanish and Portuguese New World.

However, a major precedent was set by the greatest foe of several popes, the Holy Roman Emperor Frederick II: in 1224 he created the first State university at Naples. Driven not by the pursuit of theological knowledge but by the practical need for jurists and governmental administrators, he chose to create an entirely new institution, not built on existing ecclesiastic schools. This meant his students were under less influence from the hostile Church, and were not dependent on education in Bologna, which was also hostile towards Frederick. The Catholic Church remained the main benefactor for most universities, but State funding was taken up elsewhere, as at Siena. Frederick II also set the stage for other monarchs to create universities (albeit with papal permission), such as at Valladolid in Spain and Heidelberg in Germany. The University of Paris having been in existence since the eleventh or twelfth century, it remained the model for Heidelberg in 1386. Little had changed – students were still typically teenagers, and the main subjects were still law and theology, alongside medicine and philosophy. Study at university typically took between six and twelve years. Academic freedom carried a literal meaning – as set up by Bologna, it was the right of students to safe passage in Christian kingdoms, and later, by papal bull, all those who were granted degrees had the right to teach anywhere. Still, these early universities increased access to Islamic learning and the availability of Latin translations of the ancient Greek texts, with the notable exception of Plato. The main

The religious habits worn by the teacher and students in these 1614 illustrations from Salamanca University show the monastic influence on education

Thomas Aquinas instructs a group of young clerics, thirteenth century

method of learning was known as scholasticism, a method by which a question or problem would be posed and then attacked or defended alternately, in an attempt to reach conciliations and remove contradictions, perhaps similar to the style used in Plato's Academy. Although capable of academic rigour, scholasticism could also limit intellectual exploration – it was used to advance and defend many Church teachings, but could be equally dogmatic in supporting the classics, especially Aristotle.

Ironically, it was a graduate of Frederick II's University of Naples, Thomas Aquinas, who went on to become the undisputed master of theological scholasticism and the most important thinker for the Catholic Church. As the power and wealth of the monasteries and religious orders grew, these institutions sought greater control of the universities they funded. All the while, more of the ancient Greek and Roman texts were being translated into Latin. The result was a divergence of scholarship – at Oxford, Friar Ockham (of Ockham's razor) suggested that reason and faith should be treated separately, while other scholars

The Scottish theologian and philosopher Duns Scotus, who died in 1308

such as Duns Scotus and Roger Bacon began to expand upon scientific and theological texts in new ways.

A little later, in the fourteenth and fifteenth centuries, the Byzantine Empire fell to the Ottomans, and scholars from the Hellenic tradition fled west, primarily to Italy. With them, they brought and revived Islamic and ancient Greek knowledge and texts, which were quickly taken up by the Italian universities and the wealthy city states. Plato's works were finally reintroduced, bringing contrast to Aristotle and a new Platonic Academy at Florence. Here, Renaissance Humanism developed, in objection to scholasticism. While scholasticism sought to give a few men a practical preparation for the law, medicine or Church, renaissance humanists sought to enrich their citizens – both male and female – intellectually and morally by teaching them the humanities. The movement was started primarily by churchmen and lawyers, graduates of the universities, and received enthusiastic endorsement from a succession of popes. With the mechanisation of the printing press, renaissance humanism

Guttenberg inspects the first sheet of his Bible, which has just come off the new press, c. 1440

HOUSE WHERE LUTHER DREW UP THE ARTICLES,

Luther's home at Wittenberg, where he drew up the Ninety-Five Theses

Luther nailed the Ninety-Five Theses to the door of All Saints' Church in Wittenberg

quickly spread northwards through Europe, and met with the scientific and theological legacy of the British scholars Duns Scotus, Roger Bacon, Robert Grosseteste and Sacra Bosco, and the highly influential German scholar Albert of Cologne, who spread his teachings throughout Germany and in Paris. Also in Germany, at Wittenberg University, Martin Luther began questioning the teachings and corruption of the Catholic Church, eventually writing 'The Ninety-Five Theses on the Power and Efficacy of Indulgences'. In 1517, this sparked the Protestant Reformation across most of northern Europe, spreading renaissance ideas and inventions. The printing press was one such invention, enabling a vast increase in education and manuscript production.

In many places the Reformation decreased the centralised power of the Church over the operation of universities. One of the most crucial aspects of the Reformation was the translation of the Bible. Martin Luther and his collaborators made a translation into German, and other regional translations soon followed across Europe. This democratised religion and learning – it was no longer the preserve of those educated to read Latin – and it also spelt the beginning of the end for the interoperability of education across Europe. Until this point, education had been entirely in Latin, but the long road towards the use of local languages effectively began at this point. Nevertheless, Latin remained dominant for some time, and played an important role well into the eighteenth century, Isaac Newton's *Philosophiæ Naturalis Principia Mathematica* (1687) and Carl Linnaeus's *Systemae Naturae* (1768) being notable examples of the continued importance of Latin to scholars.

While the Reformation brought developments in universities, the reaction by the Catholic Church – the Counter-Reformation or Catholic Revival – was also influential. The Jesuits in particular were instrumental in trying to integrate renaissance humanism and

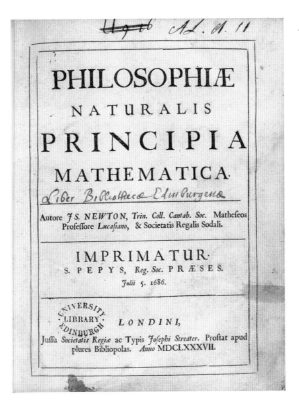

Title page of Newton's *Principia*

A page from Copernicus' *De Revolutionibus Orbium Caelestium*

Sixteenth-century caricature showing the Jesuits moving Pope Leo X forward against Martin Luther

Catholic scholasticism, as well as trying to increase the general level of education and training of priests. By the mid-sixteenth century, the Jesuits were operating over seventy colleges. The sixteenth century also saw the start of the 'scientific revolution', often associated with the seminal astronomical works of Copernicus and the anatomical work of Vesalius, both published in 1543. As the effects of the Reformation, Counter-Reformation, scientific revolution and the gradual increase of population in Europe converged, many new universities were being built, under several different guises, funding mechanisms and names. One of these, a small college in Edinburgh's Old Town, was to become the University of Edinburgh.

## THE UNIVERSITY OF EDINBURGH – A BRIEF HISTORY

### Foundation and early years

There were several motivations for the establishment of a university in Edinburgh. At the time of the foundation of the Tounis College or 'town's college' in 1583, England had just two universities, in Oxford and Cambridge. Scotland already had St Andrews (founded in 1413), Glasgow (1451) and Aberdeen (1495), all of which were set in bishops' burghs and were rooted in the Catholic Church. As noted above, it was not uncommon for young Scots to be sent abroad to study, rather than to England or to the existing pre-Reformation universities in Scotland.

The Protestant reformers of 1560 were certain of the priorities needed to establish a godly nation. The *First Book of Discipline*, a programme of reform compiled in late 1560 and adopted by the General Assembly of the new Protestant Kirk but not by Parliament, had clear aims. The longest section in it was that on education, and the wordiest part of that section was that on the 'great schools' or universities. It was the key to the reformers' aim to establish an all-graduate ministry. Yet their ambitions for the universities were hamstrung by two factors: one was the lack of funding for the whole of the programme of the new Kirk; and the other was the conservatism of the curriculum, which had scarcely changed, either in content or teaching methods, from the former Catholic universities.

By the second half of the 1570s, a new generation of reformers had replaced that of John Knox (1514–72). The foremost figure amongst a new stricter, now Presbyterian strain of Calvinism was Andrew Melville (1545–1622), an academic trained in Paris who was appointed as Principal of Glasgow University in 1574. In 1580, he moved to St Andrews to take on the post of Principal of St Mary's College. His aim was to reorganise it as the major seminary in Scotland for the training of ministers. One part of the story of the founding of the Tounis College in Edinburgh was the determination of Melville's followers, led by the first minister of Edinburgh, James Lawson, to found a college as a school of divinity along similar lines to Melville's at St Mary's. Another strand was the strife-torn politics of Edinburgh itself, which saw a bitter struggle between radicals and moderates for control of the burgh council. By early 1583, on the basis of an enabling royal charter of 1582, plans were laid for the opening of a college as a divinity school. But by the time the college opened in October of that year, a rival town council had seized power and transformed the plans for the new college. Instead, it was to follow the traditional curriculum of a *studium generale*. By 1584, Lawson was in exile in England, where he died. The town council was one of the earliest victims of the struggle within Scotland between radical Presbyterianism and a more pragmatic, sometimes Erastian view which held that the sins of Christians should be punished by civil authority, not by the Church.

A statue depicting John Knox stands in the New College quad

Common to both parties was a desire to establish a godly nation. And, in this century above all others, when literacy was increasing and the printing press was becoming a key weapon of both Calvinism and Counter-Reformation Catholicism, godliness strongly implied a humanist agenda. The catechism, read and learned by rote, became the training manual of the new religion. Yet education was also the ambition of the new 'middling sort' in society, whether lairds who acquired new lands and a new security of tenure, the new professions or merchants benefiting from a sharp increase in trade. One of the motives of both factions vying for control of Edinburgh's town council was to enable young men to be educated in Scotland rather than travelling abroad or, better still, to be schooled locally. Yet there were also perils with this agenda. Students at this time were all boys, and, as their average age was only fourteen, sending one's son away

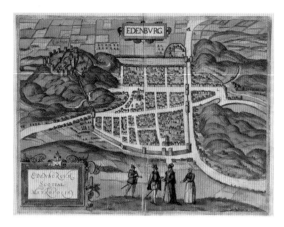

Braun's map of Edinburgh was
produced around 1580–4

A Victorian print from 1847–54
showing Holyrood Palace

to study was not only expensive but risky; students across Europe had a bad reputation for drunkenness, whoring and brawling. From the outset, the Edinburgh council was determined to exercise a strict policing of its scholarly adolescents.

The context for the new college was very different from that of the three existing Scottish universities, each of which was situated in the centre of a bishop's diocese. The population of the town of St Andrews was probably considerably less than 3,000 when the university there was first founded. Glasgow in 1451 would not have been much larger. And the bishop's burgh of Old Aberdeen, where King's College was located, had fewer than 1,000 people living in it throughout the sixteenth century and beyond. By contrast, Edinburgh in the 1580s had a population of over 14,000. Its importance as well as its population was growing rapidly. From 1579 onwards, the young king and the royal court were in near-permanent residence at the Palace of Holyroodhouse. Meetings of both Parliament and the General Assembly were almost invariably held in Edinburgh. Both the criminal and civil law courts and the royal administration were increasingly centralised in the burgh, which had laid claim to be the nation's capital since the

reign of James III (1460–88). It was not surprising that the capital of a burgeoning nation state should be intent on creating and controlling an institution which would educate a new generation of bureaucrats for the state as well as ministers for the Church.

The first students arrived on 10 October 1583. It was a very muddled and inauspicious start – the new town council appointed just two weeks after the college opened decided to overhaul arrangements made by its predecessor. The newly appointed Principal, Robert Rollock, kept his job but his job description was drastically altered. The college began its existence at Kirk o' Field with an unspecified number of students, one teacher, makeshift premises and no agreed curriculum. Under close supervision by the town council and dependent solely on public funding at that stage, money was an issue from the outset, with teaching staff paid just a fraction of what they might earn in the ministry. Local taxes imposed in part to help fund the college are likely to have set many townspeople against it, but by the 1630s private charitable funds began to support the college, although most donors, perhaps unsurprisingly in the age of the Covenants, stipulated that their support went to the teaching of theology. Curiously, the Union of the Crowns in 1603 appears to have had little impact on the Tounis College. The long-awaited return of the king, now titled King James VI of Scotland and First of England, came in 1617. If the college had hopes of royal support, it was disappointed; the king's sole gift was the title of 'King James's College'. The college spurned the honour for almost seventy years.

There is little detailed information on what was taught in the early years. The boundary between the town's grammar school and the college was somewhat blurred, but there is some evidence that Latin, Greek grammar, logic, rhetoric, arithmetic and geography were all taught. One tutor took a class through all four years of study and in all subjects; there was little concept of academic specialism until late in the seventeenth century. Variously referred to as masters or regents, teachers were paid a small stipend augmented by fees paid direct to them by students. The sons of Edinburgh residents paid £2 a year; those from further afield paid £3. A large number of would-be students turned up on 1 October 1583 but many failed a Latin language test a few days later, and in many ways the college seems to have performed the function of a secondary school, filling in gaps in students' knowledge occasioned by poor schooling in their

In contrast to the inadequate
facilities available at the Tounis
College, Leiden's library was clearly
well-established by the seventeenth
century

earlier years. Student numbers are difficult to ascertain, and studies
were interrupted periodically by outbreaks of the plague. In 1587, the
college produced forty-seven graduates, but after an initial flurry of
enthusiasm, numbers of graduates seem to have stabilised at around
twenty-five a year for some time, rising to an average of thirty-six in
the 1630s. Drop-out rates – at least from the 1630s when information
on entrant numbers started to be available – were very high, at anything up to 64 per cent.

To sum up the early years, the college was certainly not recognisable as a 'university' as might be defined today; it was a small,
ill-funded institution, with inadequate library facilities and was essentially teaching school-level subjects to a relatively small number
of boys.

### The University emerges

The seventeenth century in northern Europe is sometimes called the
'century of the city' in which a new cosmopolitan culture developed
alongside a rise in urban populations, the growth of the professions
and the consolidation of the civic hierarchy. Edinburgh first dubbed
itself a 'city' in 1606 and it did so by explicit reference to its college.
By the 1680s, Edinburgh had embraced a new kind of civic culture. It

was no longer a burgh dominated by its trading merchants. It was a city for professionals with a marked concentration of wealthy lawyers who collectively owned more assets than the rest of its inhabitants put together. It had developed a service sector which was becoming more important economically than the export and import trade on which the city (including its port of Leith) had hitherto depended for its success. Rival bodies like the College of Physicians (which acquired royal chartered status in 1681) and the College of Surgeons (which monopolised the teaching of anatomy by 1694) possibly prompted adoption of the title 'University', which was first used in 1685. A growing interest in experimental science was evident with the appointment of James Gregory as professor of mathematics in 1674 and his nephew David in 1683; teaching of Newtonian philosophy was also an Edinburgh speciality, and further changes expanded the subjects available.

According to a 1668 set of regulations, the core mission of the University was the inculcation of 'faith and good manners'. King James VII (James II of England) was resident in Edinburgh for much of the

View from Calton Hill across the Old Town and Castle

time from 1679 to 1681, and in 1688 both the royal burgh and the now retitled 'King James's University' received new charters. Royal patronage gave the University the right to grant degrees in subjects including philosophy, languages, theology, law and medicine. At the same time, the Lord Provost of Edinburgh was made Chancellor of the University, thereby thwarting attempts by the Bishop of Edinburgh to control the college. The Principal of the University became Vice-Chancellor. Both Lord Provost and Principal were attached to the royal court, but with the Glorious Revolution in 1688, James VII deposed by Parliament the following year and the crown transferring to William and Mary, State interference in all universities increased. An act of parliament in 1690, aimed at purging academia of Episcopalians and moderate Presbyterians – those who refused to take an oath of allegiance to the king and to subscribe to the Presbyterian Church – put in place a visitation of all universities. The visitation committee which examined Edinburgh's university dismissed Principal Alexander Monro and four other masters. Dr Gilbert Rule, one of the inquisitors, was appointed as Principal the day after Monro's dismissal, in an attempt to transform the University into a strict Presbyterian college. It was almost as if the original scheme of 1582 for a strict Presbyterian seminary had found its moment.

### The Scottish Enlightenment

The majority of Scots wanted to see Presbyterianism restored after the revolution of 1690 but William, as nominal head of the Church of England, needed to maintain his support for episcopacy. With advice from William Carstares, a compromise was reached and a moderate Presbyterianism was established in Scotland. The General Assembly of the Church of Scotland met in 1690 for the first time in almost forty years. With the change of monarch and the replacement of the Catholic-sympathetic James VII and II by the Protestant William, the town council sought to develop the college as an 'illustrious school', petitioning the crown for funds for a number of developments – the establishment of chairs of law and medicine, expansion of library holdings, purchase of mathematical instruments and repairs to buildings. However, the new Privy Council instead favoured turning the University into a seminary for the training of Presbyterian clergy, a project driven largely by Principal Rule. Anxious to rid the University of men who failed to take the oath of allegiance, Rule was responsible for the departure of a number of staff. At the same time, there was a lengthy period of student unrest. There is no record of any single factor which led to the unrest; perhaps it was simply a natural product of large numbers of teenage boys living in uncontrolled accommodation during a period of political and religious turmoil. An attempt by the town council in 1701 to impose a code of conduct on students failed miserably. When Rule died in 1701, he left the college in a sorry state; it was neither the 'illustrious school' the town council had wanted, nor the Presbyterian seminary desired by the Privy Council. Student numbers dwindled significantly, and as regents and professors were dependent to a large extent on the fees paid by individual students, they experienced real financial hardship.

William Carstares, painted by William Aikman

The drop in student numbers was no doubt caused in part by the college's failure to deliver a modern education, but it was also due to the fashion in the 1690s for the Edinburgh elite to send their sons to Leiden and Utrecht where they would be educated in 'polite' subjects – languages, fine arts and music – followed in many cases by the 'grand tour' of France and Italy. But the Dutch

Leiden University in the early seventeenth century

A class in progress in the fencing
hall at Leiden in 1610

This well-established anatomy
lecture hall at Leiden contrasts with
the makeshift facilities at Edinburgh
at the time, 1610

universities were an expensive option, and some had ceased to teach
in Latin, the *lingua franca* of scholarship. The town council, perhaps
spotting a market opportunity after Rule's death, licensed teachers

to cover the sciences and law. Some teachers styled themselves 'professor', and some offered the subjects a gentleman needed, including fencing, dancing and the language skills for the grand tour. Several teachers set up private academies, potentially in competition with the less than impressive University.

The town council then decided that reform of the University was needed, and between 1703 and 1726 the entire curriculum was overhauled. The system of regents – a single teacher taking an entire cohort through all subjects over the four years of study – was abolished, to be replaced by the Leiden system, where a single professor took responsibility for just one part of the curriculum. William Carstares had succeeded Rule as Principal, and was largely responsible for setting this radical overhaul in train, though he died in 1715 before it was completed. His bold move set Edinburgh apart as an enlightened university, not just well placed to educate the Scottish professional classes but also able to attract students from England too. Under Carstares, specialisms emerged. The college now offered a two-year core course in the classics followed by two years of philosophy, prior to professional study of divinity, law or medicine.

Meantime, Edinburgh was changing as a city. The College of Physicians, the Faculty of Advocates and the Surgeons' Incorporation were interested in working with the University to develop professional education in Edinburgh, and there was now sufficient

Students were issued with class tickets which allowed entry to classes held by specified professors. From left to right, these are for Professor Alexander Monro's anatomy class of 1785; 'clinical lectures' at the Royal Infirmary in 1770; and classes at the Royal Infirmary for the 1825–6 session (Charles Darwin's class card)

critical mass to retain the sons of the gentry and professional classes in Edinburgh rather than seeing them study abroad. The establishment of the medical faculty in 1726 and of the Royal Infirmary
as a teaching hospital saw further development of the University
through the provision of anatomy teaching and dissection, but much
other teaching still seems to have been a mixture of the fairly basic
school-level Latin and Greek combined with a range of subjects from
moral philosophy through to mathematics, chemistry and civil law.
Appointment of professors was still heavily influenced by political
and religious considerations, but careful political positioning had its
benefits, enabling the University to secure an annual grant of £300
from the Privy Council. Many professors were also practitioners in
their own fields of law, medicine, surgery or theology, and as such
mixed with fellow professionals across the city. This strengthened the
University's links with clubs and learned societies, with individual
professors increasingly seeing themselves as having significant public
profile. Students, meantime, developed their own societies, some
of which are still in existence today; the Royal Medical Society was
established in 1727, the Dialectic Society in 1787 and the Diagnos-
tic Society in 1816. Several societies were later grouped together as
the 'Associated Societies'. There was a growing sense of an academic
community in Edinburgh, despite the lack of any infrastructure of
buildings or residential accommodation.

The Jacobite Rising of 1745 threw Edinburgh into confusion for
a time. Many citizens left the city, college classes were cancelled,
the Court of Session adjourned and banks and businesses ceased
trading. Some of those who stayed on in the city worked to improve
the town's defences, and the college students formed their own
company of volunteers. Once the immediate concerns were over,
Edinburgh's professional classes pondered the developments they
wanted to see for their city. Numerous clubs and learned societies
were established, enabling citizens to debate aspects of culture and
philosophy, and to plan for a modern and enlightened approach
to city life. By 1750, the University had about 600 students, half of
whom studied medicine. Edinburgh was certainly the university of
choice for many American students, enrolling around 100 prior to
the American Revolution (in comparison to Glasgow's twenty and
about sixteen at the Aberdeen colleges). John Moultrie of South
Carolina was the University's first American graduate in 1749, and

went to considerable lengths to reach Edinburgh, taking thirty-two days to cross the Atlantic. Benjamin Rush, later to be one of the signatories to the Declaration of Independence, spent two months at sea and then a week travelling from Liverpool to Edinburgh in order to study at the University. In turn, Edinburgh's international alumni went on to shape development in their own countries, founding the first two American medical schools (Philadelphia in 1765 and New York in 1767). In Edinburgh, meanwhile, new chairs were established in various fields of medicine and in the sciences over the next few decades – and, importantly for the city itself, plans for the New Town were developed.

The Battle of Prestonpans in 1745, part of the Jacobite Rebellion, as depicted by William Allan in 1854

Benjamin Rush was one of two Edinburgh alumni to sign the American Declaration of Independence

James Craig's plan for the New Town saw the development of residential accommodation which was very different from that of the Old Town. It is perhaps surprising that, with the move of Edinburgh's professional classes to the north of the Nor' Loch and away from the grimy and ramshackle streets of the Old Town, plans for a new college building should nevertheless be drawn up for the original site to the south of the Old Town. Having reformed the curriculum and made the University a

Signing the American Declaration
of Independence, 4 July 1776, as
painted by John Trumbull; two of
the signatories, Benjamin Rush
and John Knox Witherspoon, were
Edinburgh alumni

world leader, Principal Robertson now led the campaign to replace
the University's disgraceful buildings at Kirk o' Field with something
more appropriate to its growing status. He started his campaign
in 1768 with a 'Memorial Relating to Edinburgh University'. He
contrasted the 'neglected state' of the University fabric, which he
saw as 'a dishonour to the City of Edinburgh and to this part of the
Country' with the flourishing University which comprised twenty-
one professors and between 600 and 700 students. His proposal was

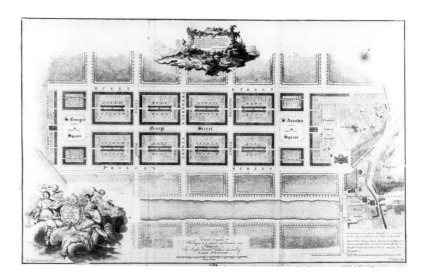

James Craig's plan of the first New
Town, 1768

for an entirely new building, at a cost of £15,000, to be funded by public subscriptions.

It was twenty years before work got properly under way, by which time North Bridge had been built, linking the Old Town to the New. Robert Adam, at the height of his architectural career, produced grand plans for an impressive building facing onto South Bridge. It would have two quadrangles and would contain public lecture rooms, a library and museum, private rooms for professors and a great hall. Across the street, a crescent of fine houses for staff – together with the civilised infrastructure of assembly rooms, a coffee house and a book shop – would serve to create a cultural hub. Notably, the plans did not include any provision for student accommodation, but the development would provide the most magnificent public building in Scotland, at a cost of £63,000. It didn't happen.

What was eventually achieved was much of what we see today in Old College, the building of which is covered more fully in Chapter 3. The foundation stone was laid on 16 November 1789 and £30,000 was raised by public subscription within the first six years of the project. However, the sudden death of Adam in 1792 and Robertson the following year left the project in disarray, leaderless and under-funded. Work on the new buildings stopped in 1794, leaving the University in a worse state than it had been prior to work starting. The Enlightenment had provided an excellent foundation for an academic institution, student and staff numbers had grown very satisfactorily, but in terms of its physical presence, the University was in a woeful state.

### Physical presence and academic development

The French Wars meant that any prospect of government funding had disappeared; by 1815 the college's annual income was only £9,000, which was less than the cost of salaries and bursaries, and there was clearly no surplus for any development work. However, successful lobbying by the Lord Provost, Sir John Marjoribanks, persuaded the British government to pay for the completion of a scaled-down project at a cost of £10,000 per annum for seven years. Under the architect William Playfair, building work started again in 1817. The scaled-down project – much as is seen in Old College today – was essentially completed by 1827. Meantime, student numbers expanded dramatically, with over 2,000 students matriculating in 1825 and many more students making short visits to the college. Medical students accounted for a high proportion of the total student numbers, with an increasing emphasis on practical education. These numbers – though very low compared with the present day – placed Edinburgh as one of the largest universities in Europe.

In 1825, a visitation committee was appointed to investigate all of the Scottish universities. The committee – the first visitation since the religiously motivated one of 1690 – found that Edinburgh's college was haphazard, lacking any proper procedures for matriculating, recording attendance or examining students. The visitors recommended that the college should aim to produce professional men who were scholars and gentlemen, and who had passed an entrance examination in the classics – a move which would have excluded most of the poor and would have had a serious impact on student numbers. After some negotiation, the visitors eventually recommended breaking the link between University and town council by establishing a rectorial court 'of intelligent and well-educated persons' to govern the University. However, nothing was put in place until 1858, when control of the University was taken away from the town council for the first time and the University Court, chaired by a Rector elected by the students, was established. Despite the delays between the visitation and the changes implemented in 1858, the educational system in place at Edinburgh over this period was widely admired and imitated across Europe and America, with its links between city and college, practice and philosophy, and learning and public life.

The remainder of the nineteenth century saw the University adapting to many external pressures. Royal commissions in 1826 and 1876 drew up plans for reform which prescribed changes and encouraged a degree of uniformity across the Scottish universities. Edinburgh was strongly Scottish, with all its professors born in Scotland, though an increasing number of students came from abroad. The University was housed in a single building – Old College – though botany lectures took place at the Botanic Garden in Inverleith Row. There were no social spaces for staff or students, and no catering facilities; students lived with their families or in lodgings. Many students were still only fifteen or

John Hope, professor of botany, taught at the Botanic Gardens; John Kay depicts him conferring with one of his gardeners

sixteen when they arrived, some of them accompanied by a guardian, and many had only a basic education. Students collected class certificates as they progressed through the years, but the concept of 'graduation', certainly in the arts, was rare and the majority of students studied part-time or short-term, often moving elsewhere after a couple of years. In 1842, the Senatus introduced a BA degree with lower requirements than the MA, but by the 1860s only about a dozen students took the MA each year, and fewer than that took the BA. For medicine, however, graduation was important, with the degree taking four years. The student cohort appears to have fallen into two reasonably distinct types; local (or at least Scottish) students were often very young and relatively ill-educated on admission, whilst those from further afield were often ambitious and well-connected, making the most of the opportunities the city provided to mix socially with some of the most influential men of the day. Debates about raising the entrance age and defining the boundary between school and university education continued.

The University's annual income from the state was about £7,800 from 1858 onwards, with all but a few hundred pounds of this going on salaries. There was nothing available for development or building work, though the government did provide some funding for the new medical school, as it had for the building of Old College. Wide-scale philanthropic giving commenced with a campaign appeal to graduates and others, and two organisations were set up in 1864, the Edinburgh University Club and the Association for the Better Endowment of the University of Edinburgh. Many donors preferred to attach their names to a prize fund or bursary, which helped individual students but not the University *per se*. Some wealthy donors were prepared to endow chairs. Honours degrees were set up in four areas – classics, mathematics, philosophy and natural science. Students had to complete the three-year curriculum first before their honours studies, but in practice there was little concept of specialisation. At the same time, standardisation of the medical curriculum across the UK and a linking of 'medicine' with 'surgery' saw the creation of the four-year MB ChB, and training in law was also 'professionalised'. Professorships in a variety of subjects were founded through individual endowments or public appeals – Sanskrit in 1862 by John Muir, a retired Indian civil servant; political economy in 1871 by the Merchant Company; and Celtic,

This plaque commemorates the University's first Chinese graduate in 1855

funded through a public appeal. Meantime, school education was progressing well with the establishment of a number of day schools in Edinburgh such as George Watson's, Daniel Stewart's and George Heriot's. More systematised schooling and the introduction by the Scotch Education Department (SED) of a Leaving Certificate allowed the University to narrow the age range of its intake, with the majority of 'bajans' – first-year students – from 1890 onwards coming in at the age of seventeen or eighteen.

The University celebrated its tercentenary in 1884 – a year late, but delayed to coincide with the opening of the new medical school, for which the then Principal, Sir Alexander Grant, had been the main fundraiser. The development of the 'New Buildings' signalled a major expansion of the University's estate, and is covered in Chapter 3.

### Changing demographics and the twentieth century

By the late nineteenth century, students were drawn from all sectors of society though predominantly from the professional and richer business classes. Around 70 per cent of students at this time were Scots by birth, although the proportion of students from outside Scotland increased over the years with significant numbers coming from South Africa, India, Australia and New Zealand, and smaller numbers coming from the United States, Canada and China.

Chinese students produced their own newsletter in 1921

Vol. I.—No. 1
[Second Edition]

中國學生雜誌

愛丁堡中國學生會出版

THE CHINESE STUDENT

OFFICIAL ORGAN OF THE EDINBURGH CHINESE STUDENTS' UNION.

JUNE 1921.

Price: One Shilling and Sixpence.

The Universities Act 1889 provided for the admission of women to universities, though Edinburgh's first female students were not admitted until 1892. In 1869, a group of female students succeeded in matriculating but were refused access to most classes; instead, they opened an independent School of Medicine for Women in 1886, working for qualifications given by the Royal Colleges. Full membership of the University medical faculty was not opened up to women until the First World War. Numbers of female students increased steadily, but the majority restricted themselves to the arts subjects, teaching being the only profession properly open to women at this time.

Bad behaviour on the part of students had continued to be an issue, as it had been from the earliest years, but in 1884 a group of students founded the Students' Representative Council (SRC). The SRC became the recognised representative body for students, providing a focus for student organisations and with input to the governance of the University. This move appears to have improved behaviour considerably, with Principal Grant praising the input of the 'student element' to the tercentenary and referring to them as a 'corporate body'. Another major development at this time was the building of the University Union, which is covered in Chapter 8.

The governance structure put in place in 1889 is effectively still in use today. The Court, chaired by the Rector and his appointee 'assessors', and with members from the town council, took over financial responsibility. The Senatus, chaired by the Principal and consisting of all the professors, determined the University's academic direction and administration. A new body, the General Council, had been established in 1858. It comprised all graduates of the University and the professors. Between the SRC and the General Council, students present and past now had a say in the way their University functioned.

During the first half of the twentieth century, the University settled into what might be quite recognisable now as a traditional university – teaching a wide range of subjects in a structured degree hierarchy to students from a variety of social backgrounds, both sexes and many nationalities. At the same time, academic staff were increasingly engaging in their own research alongside their teaching functions. By the start of the Second World War, Edinburgh was admitting around 1,000 students per annum and had moved to a system of three terms, thereby increasing the teaching year from a paltry twenty weeks (from late October to the end of March, with just a short break at Christmas) to thirty weeks from October to June. The balance between lectures (which were always delivered by professors) and tutorial and laboratory work changed, with increasing emphasis on the practical.

In 1919, the University acquired a greenfield site at Liberton, and started the construction of the King's Buildings science campus. The first department to open there was chemistry in 1922, followed

Cowan House (seen here around 1948–50) provided residential accommodation for male students

by zoology (1929) and geology (1932). Other subjects utilised the old High School Yards opposite Old College, much of this physical expansion being funded through a combination of public appeals and donations from generous benefactors. The post-war interest in

The animal genetics building soon after its opening in 1930

Sir Basil Spence, architect of the Main Library

physical fitness and games was given a major boost by Sir Donald Pollock (1868–1962), who had graduated in medicine in 1893 but made his fortune in industry. He bought and donated land in the Pleasance for a new gymnasium, and in 1942–3 gave the land on which Pollock Halls of Residence were later built. At this time, the University was still largely non-residential, though Masson House and Cowan House in George Square provided some accommodation for women and men respectively. The University opened Cowan House in 1929 using funds donated by shipowner Thomas Cowan of Leith, in gratitude for volunteer efforts by students during the General Strike of 1926.

West Mains Road in 1935, prior to extensive development of the King's Buildings site

The chemistry building, around 1948–50

The zoology building, around 1948–50

The second half of the twentieth century saw a massive expansion of the UK university system. New 'plate glass' campus-based universities were established in a number of locations across the UK, and government funding was pumped into the existing universities to enable expansion on an unprecedented scale. At Edinburgh, much of this was channelled into George Square, with the demolition of much of the fine but admittedly run-down Georgian square and its replacement with the Appleton Tower, Main Library, David Hume Tower, William Robertson Building and Adam Ferguson Building. At King's Buildings there was also major expansion. Like the majority of buildings of that era, these have not necessarily aged well, and a programme of major refurbishment has been necessary.

Subject choice continued to expand – Edinburgh was the first university to create a chair in nursing (in 1971) – and other significant changes included the incorporation of the Edinburgh Dental School in 1948, the merger with the Royal (Dick) School of Veterinary Studies in 1951, Moray House School of Education in 1998 and Edinburgh

College of Art in 2011. Sadly, the dental school – Scotland's first facility for the training of dentists and dating back to 1856 – fell prey to government cuts in the late 1980s. Despite vigorous campaigning, it proved impossible to win the argument that there was a need for more than one dental school in Scotland, and the final cohort of undergraduates qualified in 1994, exactly 100 years after the Edinburgh Dental Hospital and School had moved to its Chambers Street premises. Dentistry does, however, retain a presence in Edinburgh; in 1997, the Edinburgh Dental Institute opened in purpose-built premises in Lauriston Place, providing postgraduate training and research facilities.

The Main Library, Appleton Tower and David Hume Tower, from the Meadows

Student funding over four centuries has moved from wholly private to a mixture of private and philanthropic, to state-funded through the erstwhile student grant system and now back to a mixed system (supported, for UK students, through public loan schemes and for students from Scotland by the government). Student numbers have continued to rise – the 31,000 students registered in 2012–13 is more than double the entire population of Edinburgh and Leith in the 1580s – and the recent introduction of Massive Online Open Courses (MOOCs) has already seen over 900,000 people taking up the opportunity to sample university-level education.

From an inauspicious start over 400 years ago, the University has matured into a world-class institution unrecognisable from the early days of the Tounis College except, perhaps, for some important underlying principles. Set up to inculcate 'faith and good manners',

The interior of the dental school, around 1948–50

the University today encourages students to have faith in their abilities and the good manners to apply them for the benefit of society through their careers. From the vision and high ideals of its founders through to current plans for the future, the University is confidently moving through its fifth century as a modern institution contributing on a truly global level, whilst still firmly rooted in the 'town' to which it belongs.

Edinburgh College of Art merged
with the University in 2011

The merger with ECA has brought new and colourful events
to the University, as with this fashion show in the Playfair Library

# 3

## Building the University

WITH OVER 350 ACADEMIC BUILDINGS in the city and building stock ranging in date from 1618 to 2014, the University of Edinburgh is a major contributor to the urban landscape in what is a World Heritage Site. Few universities in the UK have a higher number of listed buildings (buildings of architectural importance) than Edinburgh, and responsibility for such a heritage falls to Estates and Buildings on a daily basis. Not all of the University's listed buildings are particularly old; the Main Library and the David Hume Tower in George Square are both examples of iconic 1960s design and have been listed comparatively recently. Listing brings with it restrictions on alteration and repairs, additional costs due to requirements for particular materials and major responsibilities as far as preservation of the townscape is concerned. Development of the University's portfolio of buildings has been enabled over the years by many benefactors. This chapter looks at a few examples of what has been achieved.

Stonework detail from
60 George Square

Stained glass in New College

View along Buccleuch Place

The David Hume Tower

## OLD COLLEGE

Standing squarely on the corner of Chambers Street and South Bridge, Old College has been both the symbolic and practical heart of the University for over 200 years. To the casual observer, the building looks very much 'of a piece', following classical principles of design and apparently constructed seamlessly over a concentrated period of building. However, closer examination reveals that Old College is not quite as uncomplicated as it might first appear. There are subtle differences in, for example, the detailing around windows, and this starts to reveal the somewhat chequered history of the development of the building. But before looking properly at Old College, it is worth considering the development of the University prior to that, and what Old College replaced.

From the University's foundation in 1583 as the Tounis College it was the responsibility of the town, and the town council had to find and fund basic premises and salaries. Money was always in short supply and donations, large or small, were always welcome. The college buildings were gradually built up in the seventeenth century around three irregular courtyards. Edinburgh never became a residential university in the way that the collegiate structure existed in Oxford and Cambridge, although the various new blocks were often intended originally as student chambers. A number of the professors did live in college premises but most of the new buildings were soon adapted as teaching classrooms.

The Golden Boy, reflected in the windows of Old College

The first history of the University, by Thomas Craufurd, professor of philosophy and mathematics, summarised events in the University year by year from 1580 to 1646. Information on donors relates them to different sets of chambers. Thus, for example, John Jossie, College Treasurer in the town council, built the steps linking the High and Laigh (Low) Courts and went on to fund 'the chamber above the great gate' himself, setting an example for

The carved stones mounted in the foyer of one of the lecture theatres in Old College are all that remain of the old buildings

others. There followed various chambers surrounding the Laigh College Court, funded in the 1640s by John Trotter; Robert Elise; Robert Johnson; Bailies Robert Flemine and Laurence Henderson; George Sootie, Dean of Guild; William Thomson, Clerk of the City; and James Murray. Quite a number of such donations were made by members of the town council in a private capacity.

The only physical remains of these early buildings are the small collection of sculptured stones that were rescued during the demolition of the last of the old buildings to clear the site for the building now known as Old College. These stones were built into the vestibule of the then mathematics classroom in 1827 (now the lobby outside one of the lecture theatres in the law school) and reflect the mixture of council and private funding of the old buildings. The town council had funded two major buildings, in 1617 and 1646, and there is a fine inscription recording the donation by 'Senatus Populusque Edinburgensis' of the 1617 building. Also recorded is a donation by Thomas Dods, Town Plumber, who died of the plague in 1646 and whose endowment was used for a student chamber built in 1670. Another inscription records the bequest by 'Andrew Baron Rutherford, Earl of Teviot and Governor of Tangier, an alumnus of this College, renowned both at home and abroad in the arts of war and of peace', which was used in 1664 for a terrace of four student chambers, known as the Teviot Chambers. A Latin inscription from the bell tower over the entrance gate, built around 1686, records that 'Thomas Burnet, Writer, descended from the illustrious families of Leys on the one side and Craigmyle on the other, a pious and generous man, had this bell tower built at his own expense for the service and embellishment of Town and College', adding for good measure 'Spectator – Mark, Praise and Imitate'. From its earliest days, the University was heavily dependent on the generosity of donors, and funding was to become increasingly important as the University planned its next major development.

Anyone who has made even the shortest of visits to Edinburgh will be aware of the city's 'two towns'. Edinburgh's earliest development started around the Castle, defensively placed on the crag of the spectacular crag-and-tail, a geological feature produced by ancient volcanic action followed by glaciation; the tail extends down the Royal Mile/High Street to Holyrood. The development of increasingly tall houses down each side of the Mile, separated by narrow vennels running at ninety degrees to the main street, meant that by the sixteenth century the town was crowded and unpleasant. The cramped high-rise buildings were a considerable fire risk, and the lack of light and air and the absence of basic sanitation must have made the city an unpleasant place to live in. There had of course been some development beyond the confines of the Old Town, and the University's early buildings were part of that development.

In 1766, a competition was held to design a 'New Town', to be constructed to the north of the existing town on the other side of a boggy area of land below the Castle, known as the Nor' Loch (now Princes Street Gardens). The competition was won by a young architect,

Salisbury Crags rising behind this view of the summer house at Moray House show the city's challenging topography. Oliver Cromwell is believed to have lodged at Moray House in 1651, and in the early eighteenth century negotiations leading to the Act of Union took place in the grounds of Moray House

James Craig. Building of the New Town started a few years later, and proceeded in phases until around 1830; the grid plan around Princes Street, George Street and Queen Street is still very much as envisaged by James Craig.

It might have been assumed that the up-and-coming University would choose to site its new premises in the New Town, but it did not do so. Edinburgh's development was not as simple as the 'two towns', and the siting of Old College shows how inextricably the development of the University was linked to the development of the city, and also indicates how financial exigencies may have determined location. Whilst the New Town was a spectacular and primarily residential development, the city was also spreading to the south of the Old Town, albeit in a less 'planned' way than the New Town. George Heriot's Hospital, some fine villas along what is now Chambers Street, St Cecilia's Hall and the (Old) High School are all examples of the city's expansion southwards. The development of high-quality houses around George Square (now almost entirely occupied by the University) rivalled many of those in the New Town itself. The University, meantime, was still housed in a ramshackle collection of buildings on the site of the old Kirk o' Field monastery. Many of these were

This view of the 'old library', with Adam's New Buildings rising around it, shows the woeful state of the University's premises at the turn of the nineteenth century

By contrast, Padua University had fine buildings as early as 1630

by now over 100 years old and had apparently been poorly maintained – Henry Marchant, an American visiting in 1769, described the University's buildings as 'a most miserable musty pile scarce fit for stables'. Principal Robertson first mooted reconstruction of the college in 1768, but there were no funds to enable this at the time. The town council still had full responsibility for the University's buildings and finances, but the little money which was allocated to the University was primarily for bursaries and the meagre salaries of the professors. By 1789, it was clear that a public subscription, backed by a government donation, would be needed were the University ever to achieve the new buildings it needed to match its increasing status. Meantime, development of the city was proceeding, with the building of North Bridge and later South Bridge opening up access from the south and leading to the focal point of Register House at the east end of Princes Street. Work on South Bridge started in 1786, and it was opened to foot passengers in 1788. Location of the fine new building for the University on that north/south axis was therefore not out of place; more importantly, perhaps, the University already owned the land and therefore saved on those initial purchase costs.

Robert Adam had drawn up grand plans for the southern approach to the city, including preliminary designs for new University buildings, and he was subsequently appointed to design the college building. The project, seen to be of national rather than merely civic importance, was put in the hands of trustees representing the great and the good in Scottish public life, who were to oversee the enterprise and raise the necessary funds by public appeal. The Lord Provost, Thomas Elder, and the Principal of the University, William Robertson, were closely involved in day-to-day administration, as were their successors. Adam's plan (apparently drawn around 1789 but not published until 1791) shows a fine building with a double quadrangle, the whole intended to house a chapel, hall, museum, teaching rooms, library and residential accommodation for the Principal and many of the professors. The University's students by now numbered around 1,000, but there was to be no provision for accommodation for them 'as the students live promiscuously with the other inhabitants [of the city]'.

After a lengthy gestation period, building work seemed to start quite suddenly; Principal Robertson convened a special meeting of the Senatus in October 1789 and announced that the foundation

Robert Adam's drawings for Old College, 1789

stone would be laid the following month. The Lord Provost explained to the same meeting that the town council had been encouraged by the 'prospect of a liberal contribution from the publick, and of aid from Government'. The trustees, who included Henry Dundas, the Duke of Buccleuch and the Lord Provost, resolved to advertise in London newspapers for subscriptions. They appear to have been confident that this appeal would receive wide public support; a total of £40,000 was needed. Initially all went well. Some £15,000 was raised in the next year or two. Lists of the moneys already raised were published. The city promised £400 per annum, the Writers to the Signet 200 guineas, the Faculty of Advocates and the Royal Society 100 guineas each, all these for five years. The Royal College of Physicians gave £150 and the College of Surgeons £105. Several Scottish peers gave £100 or more, and many other titled people gave sums of £50 to £100. Individual doctors and surgeons gave

The Lord Provost, Thomas Elder, is appropriately depicted by Raeburn with the plans for Old College in the background

The college museum, reputedly with a tame puma, seen here under one of the display cases

The museum became a reading room in the 1940s

The original museum space is now the Georgian Gallery

generously, as did several of the professors and many ministers of the Kirk. A few donors gave in kind – 500 bags of lime; a log of mahogany at Leith; two Highland oxen to be sold by the Deacon of the Fleshers; 40,000 slates free of charge apart from the cost of transport from the quarry at Easdale.

Just three years later, however, Robert Adam died suddenly, having set down only three corners of a great quadrangle amidst arguments over contracts with masons and carpenters and hints of dishonest dealings by some builders. Adam's death in 1792 was clearly a major setback, as was Principal Robertson's the following year, but the French Wars from 1793 to 1815 posed a bigger problem. Men and materials were diverted to Britain's war with France, inflation ran high and money was in

The foundation stone of Old College was laid in 1789

short supply. A series of poor harvests added to the national misery, and money for projects such as the building of the college was impossible to secure. Professor Andrew Duncan made specific appeals to medical graduates, at home and scattered throughout the empire, but with diminishing returns. In 1799, the trustees drew up a petition seeking government assistance to enable them to pay debts of over £5,000 to different tradesmen. In their petition, they described the woeful state of the college development; work had stopped, leaving the east and north fronts unroofed and 'the beams and joisting exposed to the injury of the weather'. Student numbers were given as 1,300, suggesting that the University had recruited successfully during this time, despite the poor state of its premises. A royal warrant of £5,000 helped clear the debts already incurred but building work was stopped with some £30,000 expended, only the new anatomy block already occupied and the great showpiece entrance facade an empty ruin, not even windproof and watertight. It is possible that the behaviour of students did not help; discipline seems to have been poor throughout this period, and a writer in 1812 noted that students 'and many other persons who are not Students' persisted in playing ball games 'by which great loss is sustained by the breaking of windows'.

View of Old College and Chambers Street in 1840

William Playfair's design for the first floor of Old College

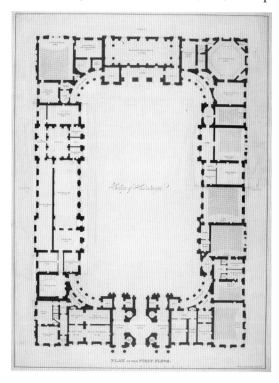

A further application to the Treasury in 1813 was also unsuccessful, but in 1815 the town council and the University jointly petitioned the government once more, and this time received an initial grant of £10,000, 'with prospect of the like sum annually for seven years'. The town council advertised a competition inviting architects to submit plans to finish the college building on a reduced scale; it was clear that economies would have to be made and Adam's plan modified, but, importantly, the competition specified 'the preservation of the architecture of Mr Adam as far as practicable'.

In 1816, new college trustees were appointed. The young William H. Playfair won the architectural competition, retaining as much as possible of Adam's plan but throwing his double courtyard design into a single quadrangle. Several extensions of the government grant allowed the completion of the Main Library on the south side of the quadrangle, but from around 1830 further grants were firmly refused and responsibility for the buildings was returned by default to the city.

The most important parts of Old College left unfinished were the addition of the dome

The Playfair Library today

over the entrance and the paving of the quadrangle. Both were eventually achieved, with the help of generous donors. Robert Cox of Gorgie, a lawyer, writer and philanthropist who died in 1872, left a bequest specifically for the erection of the dome and by 1886 the capital amounted to some £4,400. Adam's original design was more

View of Old College, looking north along South Bridge, in 1887 before the addition of the dome

Hutchison's Golden Boy, 'Youth Bearing the Torch of Knowledge'

of a small bell tower over the entrance and was not thought appropriate for Playfair's enlarged quadrangle. The plaque below Cox's bust in the room below the dome, originally the Fine Art Museum, tells the story: Cox, 'a just and generous man, a learned author, an enemy of ignorance and superstition … bequeathed the fund for the erection of this dome, a feature in the original design by Robert Adam, now built from the plans of R. Rowand Anderson, L.L.D.'. It was crowned by the statue of the Golden Boy, 'Youth Bearing the Torch of Knowledge', by John Hutchison, in 1888. The paving of the quadrangle is a much more recent development, and is covered below.

OLD COLLEGE QUAD

Spectacular as the buildings might be, the quadrangle at Old College never lived up to the promise of the buildings themselves. Used variously over the years as a car park, loading area for deliveries, bicycle storage area and just somewhere to pass through, the quad was, for many years, surfaced with a dull grey gravel which was uncomfortable to walk on and either dusty during dry weather or muddy in

By the 1880s, Edinburgh was a handsome modern city, as this view from the Castle shows

Old College quadrangle in 1900

the rain. Principal O'Shea determined, soon after taking up his post, that cars would henceforth be banned from the quad, and they were. This allowed for the arrival of some benches, but the area was still not attractive and these were not well used. All this changed in 2010 with a generous donation from a benefactor specifically to tackle the quad. Architects Simpson and Brown were commissioned, and after much historical research on what might have been intended for the quad had the money not run out in the nineteenth century, the simplest

Old College quadrangle in 2011 at the time of the Chancellor's installation

of designs was produced. The landscaping of the quad – now a plain rectangle of turf surrounded by honey-coloured Clashach sandstone hand-droved to produce a historically accurate non-slip surface – was completed in time for the inauguration of HRH The Princess Royal as Chancellor in 2011. Old College is now 'finished' after a 200-year gap in its construction, and is rightly the focal point of the University. The quad hosts official events, has been used in the Edinburgh International Festival and sees a daily stream of students and visitors. An award by the British Association of Landscape Industries (BALI) in 2012 is a tribute to the excellent design, the execution of that design by the contractors and to the foresight of the donors, without whom this work would not have been possible.

An unexpected spin-off from the work to transform the quad into one of the city's most attractive squares was the discovery of very significant archaeological remains. These will, in due course, be the subject of a major book. It had long been understood that Old College was built on the site of the old Kirk o' Field – properly, the collegiate church of St Mary in the Fields – renowned as the site of the murder in 1567 of Henry Stuart, Lord Darnley, the second husband of Mary, Queen of Scots. Whilst debate about the site of the murder continues, the archaeological dig revealed far more than had been anticipated about the city's past, and about the University's past too. The remains of Hamilton House, a mansion built in 1552 for the Duke of Chatelherault, obviously predated the establishment of the University, as did some forty skeletons from the Kirk o' Field graveyard, a number of them uncovered just inches below the surface. Perhaps of more direct relevance to the history of the University, the foundations of many of the buildings which preceded Old College were discovered, including remnants of the first library, dating back to 1617. In the north-west corner some valuable ephemera emerged. Professor Joseph Black was professor of chemistry from 1766, a key figure in the Scottish Enlightenment and the discoverer of carbon dioxide. Near his laboratory various chemicals were identified, but following a lead that some of Black's chemicals may have been stored under the old library, the walls of which had been identified, a further dig was undertaken. This revealed a collection of vessels and chemicals which has enabled further understanding of how chemistry was researched in that period. There is much more work to be done in analysing and interpreting the finds, but already the University's appreciation of what it is built

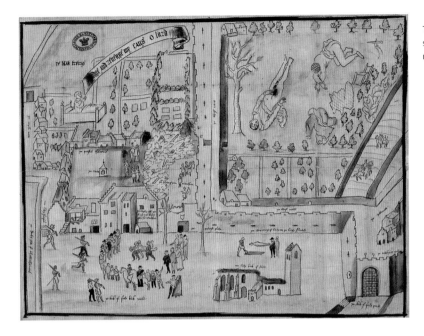
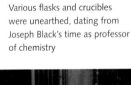

This map from 1567 depicts the scene at the Kirk o' Field after the murder of Lord Darnley

on – literally and metaphorically – has been deepened considerably. Completion of a project that began at the start of the French Revolution has added greatly to that understanding, and would not have been possible without the generosity of donors.

Archaeologists excavating the quad under the site of the Old Library had to take precautions against chemical contamination

Various flasks and crucibles were unearthed, dating from Joseph Black's time as professor of chemistry

## THE MEDICAL SCHOOL OR 'NEW BUILDINGS'

By the nineteenth century, the University had a worldwide reputation for the excellence of its teaching of medicine and surgery, intricately linked with the Royal Infirmary which had been founded in 1729, but once more development of the University was hampered by shortage of premises. The Infirmary moved from Infirmary Street to splendid new premises on Lauriston Place in 1879. Locating the new medical school buildings adjacent to the new Royal Infirmary was a logical step. Funds of £60,000 were raised through a public subscription, and an architectural competition was announced in

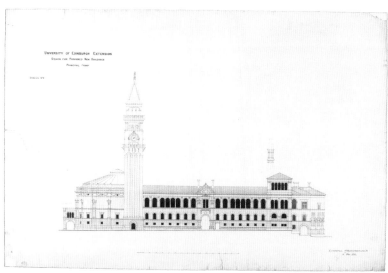

R. Rowand Anderson's drawings for the 'New Buildings' which would house the medical school

Anderson's 'Cinquecento style' façade

Plans for the medical school incorporated a long list of requirements specified by the professors

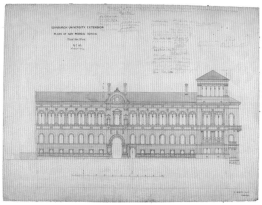

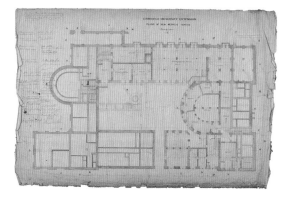

This view from 1900 shows the completed medical school, and the top of Middle Meadow Walk

The quadrangle of the medical school in 1900

1874 for development of a major area between Teviot Row, Middle Meadow Walk and George Square. As *The Scotsman* reported on 9 September that year: 'The buildings to be erected are to comprise a completely appointed Medical School, as also a College Hall, suitable for important academical gatherings'.

The announcement went on to specify in great detail the medical departments which were to be housed in the new buildings, the number of students in each department, the preference for roof lights rather than windows, the need for laboratories and an 'Anatomical Museum' and provision for cellars and courtyards. Early in 1875, it was announced that Mr Robert Anderson of Edinburgh had won the competition, adopting 'the Cinquecento style'. Robert Anderson – who later styled himself R. Rowand Anderson – designed a magnificent building incorporating the medical school, a 'great hall' and a campanile. *The Scotsman* described his choice of design as 'an intermediate between the Gothic and the stiff … Palladian', noting that the Italian cinquecento 'naturally commended itself to an architect so widely heedful of the practical, on account of its plasticity and adaptability to varied internal arrangements'. The writer quite clearly saw Old College as sadly old-fashioned at this stage.

Private funding of £25,000 was needed to secure a national grant of £80,000, which would enable the building of the 'New Buildings'. The money must have been forthcoming; by 1880, the anatomy department was occupying its new premises and work on the rest of the medical school – though without its campanile and great hall – was progressing well. But medical student numbers increased dramatically – from 900 in 1875 to 1,700 by 1882 – and plans for the

The entrance to the Anatomical Museum

medical school buildings had to be expanded, resulting in heavy additional costs. In 1884, the University launched its Tercentenary Appeal, securing £36,000 towards the cost of completion of the buildings. Sir David Baxter of Kilmaron was a major donor, bequeathing £20,000. An estimated £15,000 was still needed to complete and kit out the new buildings, and Mr William McEwan promised £5,000 of this, provided the remainder was raised from other sources. The completed buildings were formally handed over to the Senatus Academicus in October 1885.

The medical school buildings continued in unbroken use for their original purposes until the early twenty-first century, when the Royal Infirmary moved to new premises on the edge of the city and most academic departments gradually moved to the Little France site. The old medical school buildings still house various research units, and have provided a new home for two schools from the College of Humanities and Social Science.

Mr William McEwan in 1893

Students at the new medical school buildings at Little France

The McEwan Hall in 1900

## THE MCEWAN HALL

As noted above, plans for the medical school included proposals for a 'great hall' and campanile. Whilst funding never became available for the campanile, the University did achieve its great hall, which is now one of its most iconic buildings. The absence of a 'University Hall'

Anderson's drawings for the McEwan Hall

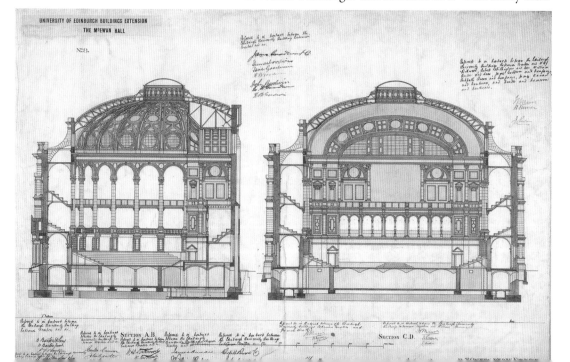

was lamented in 1874 when the campaign for the 'New Buildings' was announced; the 'degradation' of being reduced to hiring a hall for great occasions was mentioned, and Oxford's Sheldonian Theatre was held up as an example of what was proper. Those attending the public meeting were assured that the University of Edinburgh would 'shortly stand possessed of a Hall of Assembly which has no parallel elsewhere'. Luckily, 'shortly' was not defined, as it was to be over twenty years before the University realised its aims.

In the announcement of the architectural competition in 1874, specifications had been given for a flat-floored room without fixed seating, galleries with fixed seating on three sides, a 'railed orchestra' on the fourth and adopting 'the best acoustic principles'. The hall was to accommodate 2,000 people, and was to be usable for graduation and other ceremonies, as well as for examinations – hence the flat-floored room without fixed seating. A janitor's residence, a small reading room for professors, a small library and reading room for students, and a belfry were also on the wish list; and a limit of £70,000 was placed on the basic construction costs. In 1886, William McEwan – who had already donated funds for the medical school buildings – intimated that he was prepared to contribute £40,000 to enable the University to achieve its great hall. McEwan was an Edinburgh-based brewer who amassed a considerable fortune over the course of his career; he was also a Liberal Member of Parliament for four years. The current Principal jokes that it is fitting that the University holds its graduations in a hall built from profits from the sale of beer, but that is precisely what the McEwan Hall is. McEwan's already generous donation was later increased to £115,000 to enable completion of the hall. The sum of £165,000 for purchase of the entire 'New Buildings' site and for building works had come from public subscriptions. A further £88,000 came from government grants. Mr McEwan put up the money for the hall, and work started in 1888.

The upper gallery of the McEwan Hall, showing Palin's decorative scheme

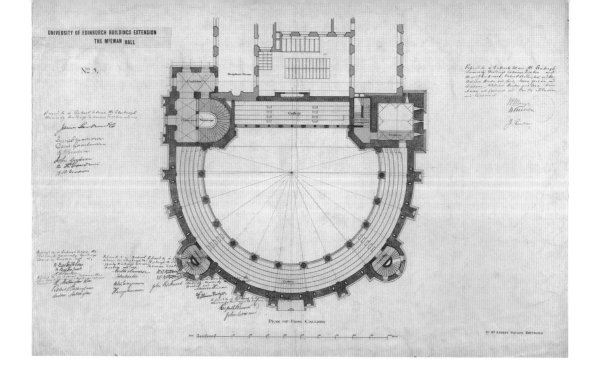

PLAN OF FIRST GALLERY

Anderson based his design on Greek theatre, claiming this had good acoustic properties

The tympanum above the main entrance to the McEwan Hall

The architect R. Rowand Anderson had included sketches for the great hall in his plans for the 'New Buildings' which would house the medical school, and with funding in place he was now able to dust them off and implement them. The exterior of the McEwan Hall may be Italianate in style, but Anderson based the design of the internal space on ancient Greek theatre, explaining what he saw as the acoustic benefits of doing so. The building itself was finished by 1894, but McEwan then instructed a lavish scheme of decoration which took

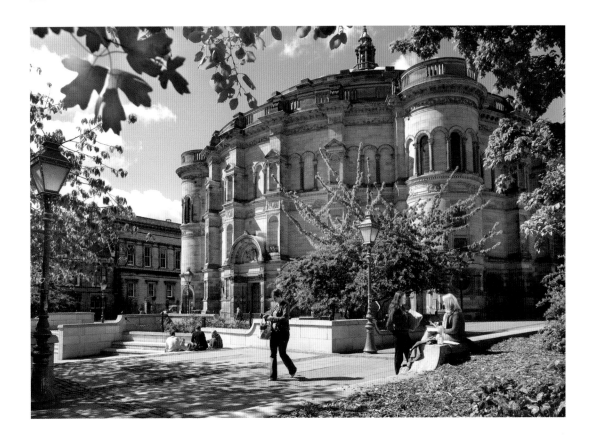

over three years to complete. The artist William Palin conceived a grand scheme which conveyed the ideal of a university at that time. Famous names connected with the University of Edinburgh, a passage of scripture and portraits of the donor himself, Sir Walter Scott and Thomas Carlyle (both alumni of Edinburgh) are all included. Above the platform, a huge painted panel entitled 'The Temple of Fame' depicts over eighty philosophers and students ascending the steps, while goddesses representing Science, Art and Literature look on. The other late addition to the McEwan Hall was the organ. It was not included in the original plan, but its incorporation extended the use of the hall still further. In recognition of William McEwan's generosity, the University awarded him the honorary degree of Doctor of Laws at the opening ceremony on 3 December 1897. The McEwan Hall, bearing an inscription on the outside acknowledging the donor's generosity, continues to be used as originally intended – for graduations and ceremonies, for examinations, and for concerts and public events.

The McEwan Hall in spring

Overleaf: The hall continues to be used for graduation ceremonies

## THE NOREEN AND KENNETH MURRAY LIBRARY, KING'S BUILDINGS

The opening of the new Murray Library in 2012 marked the culmination of a project which had been on the drawing board since 2007 and which provides an excellent example of the good use to which donations large and small can be put cumulatively. Donations of £1,000 or over came in from twenty-two people, 156 donors gave sums of up to £100 and donations over the full range between those amounts took the total raised through the campaign to over £400,000.

As noted in the opening sections of this book, the establishment of a library predated the foundation of the University by some years, thanks to Clement Litill's bequest. Libraries have obviously continued to be essential to universities over the centuries, but the modern library is a very different place from the 'collection of books: a building or room containing it' defined by *Chambers Dictionary*. The development of printing technology and the relative availability of printed books from the sixteenth century onwards led to libraries increasing in size as buildings, and to institutions priding themselves on the number of volumes in their collections. This view of libraries continued largely unchanged until very recently. The much-vaunted 'digital revolution' has, however, seen huge changes in the last ten years or so in the way libraries are used.

Information Services and the College of Science and Engineering decided that the focus of the project should be on providing a range of different types of spaces reflecting the ways that students now expect to study. It was agreed that much of the library's print book and journal collections should be placed in storage, given that their use was decreasing significantly as a result of the rapid growth in electronic provision.

The new library at King's Buildings provides computing facilities which are second to none. Future-proofing a venture of this kind requires vision and a certain amount of guesswork. Even just a decade ago, the easy availability of mobile computing was not envisaged, and a library designed at that time would probably have provided space for banks of fixed desktop computers. Now, most students have laptops, internet on a mobile phone and possibly other mobile devices too; the current need for the working library is space to sit, to plug in and recharge (literally and metaphorically), to work collaboratively with colleagues in a 'pod' and to be able to turn the results of that exercise into high-quality digitally produced output.

As well as being a library, it was agreed that the building should bring a much-needed physical and social focus to the campus. It was felt that King's Buildings lacked a 'living heart', which originated from the way that the campus had developed since the foundation stone for the chemistry building was laid by King George V in 1920. The new building therefore needed to be central to the wider strategic development of the campus and to make use of the pleasant green environment in the central zone.

The building is engineered to the best environmental standards and achieved a Building Research Establishment Environmental Assessment Method (BREEAM) 'Excellent' certification for design and procurement. Its L-shaped plan with double-height atrium produces a narrow floor plate, allowing ventilation and optimising natural light. There is a green roof and sustainable fabric has been used

The Noreen and Kenneth Murray Library at King's Buildings

throughout. Its south elevation faces the 'green heart' of the campus with a large and attractive balcony open to library users. It has been 'Highly Commended' by Carbon Trust Scotland.

The four floors provide a gradation of high-quality environments, from informal catered study and social space on the ground floor, through a range of collaborative and private study spaces on the first and second floors, to silent, individual study on the top floor. There are seven group study rooms, and the book collection is distributed across the upper three floors. Staff from Information Services deliver high-quality integrated library and IT enquiry services from the helpdesk on the first floor. The library is open in the evenings and at weekends throughout semester, and it now forms part of the distributed study space provision on campus.

From the outset, the library has been a huge success. There has been very positive feedback from staff, students and external visitors. Landscaping work was undertaken, and staff and students are now able to sit outside in good weather, which makes the centre of the campus a much more vibrant environment.

## THE ROYAL (DICK) SCHOOL OF VETERINARY STUDIES

The Dick Vet, as it is affectionately known, could legitimately feature in every chapter of this book, owing its very creation to an act of philanthropy. William Dick initially trained as a farrier at his father's forge in Clyde Street. In 1816 he attended extramural lectures in anatomy given by Dr John Barclay. Barclay saw his student's potential and was an important mentor to Dick over the coming years. The following year, Dick travelled to London to study under Professor Edward Coleman at the Veterinary College in Camden. He received his diploma in January 1818 and returned to Edinburgh to set up his own veterinary school, initially combining lecturing from a rented room with practical instruction delivered in his father's forge. Meantime, his sister Mary oversaw the finances, and kept an eye on the manners and morals of the students. Dick's own fundraising efforts, coupled with donations from himself and his sister, Mary, enabled the foundation of the Veterinary College of Edinburgh in 1823. In 1833, he planned a new building, paying £2,500 himself, with a further £50 coming from the Highland Society towards the cost of fitting out the lecture theatre and museum. Dick

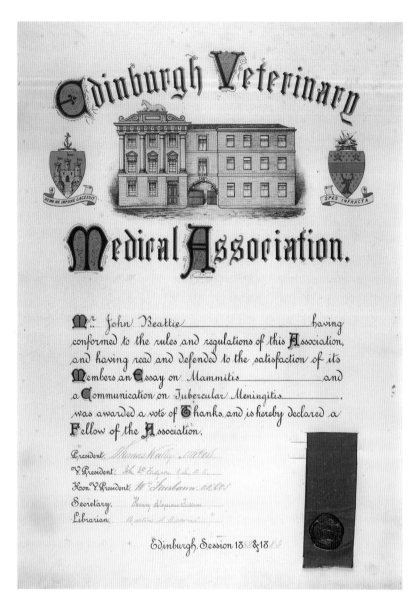

The Veterinary College was independent for many years and issued its own degree certificates; this one, for John Beattie, was awarded in 1883

continued to expand the school, buying up adjacent premises in Clyde Street as they became available. His professional reputation continued to grow; he was appointed Veterinary Surgeon in Scotland to Queen Victoria in 1844. By the time of William Dick's death in 1866, he had taught 818 students including the founders of veterinary schools in Glasgow, Liverpool, Ireland, Canada, the USA and Australia – an impressive global reach for a man who is buried a mere 100 metres from his birthplace in Whitehorse Close.

The Veterinary College was independent for many years, though it had close links to the University. Formally named the Royal (Dick) Veterinary College in 1906, it was incorporated into the University in 1951. The Dick Vet moved from its Clyde Street premises to new purpose-built premises at Summerhall in 1916, occupying those until very recently. The Summerhall complex grew to include surrounding buildings which were converted for teaching purposes, and the tower on the corner housed many of the research facilities from 1971 onwards. In 1990, questions were raised about the viability of having two veterinary schools in one small country; with just six veterinary schools in the UK, having two in Scotland was

William Dick, staff and students in the courtyard of his Clyde Street school in the early 1860s

Summerhall under construction

arguably over-provision. A similar argument had seen the decision in 1989 that the Edinburgh Dental School should be closed, and once again, the same two universities – Edinburgh and Glasgow – were both fighting to retain facilities each thought vital. Concerted campaigns by both institutions ensured the survival of both veterinary schools.

With the support of numerous donors and a major fundraising campaign, the Royal (Dick) School of Veterinary Studies moved to a new state-of-the-art home on the southern edge of Edinburgh in September 2011, in time for the start of the new academic year. Adjacent to the Roslin Institute and the Hospital for Small Animals, the teaching facility at the Dick Vet now

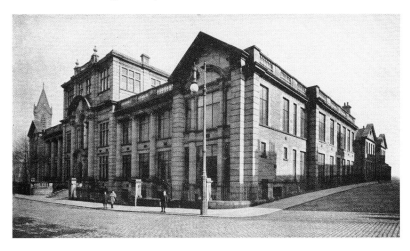

Summerhall soon after its opening in 1916

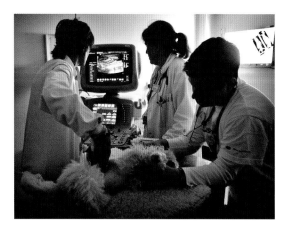

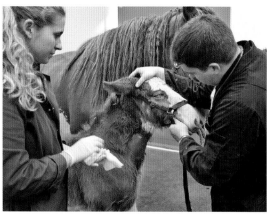

The animal hospital facilities at the new Dick Vet premises cater for a wide variety of patients

forms one of the largest communities of veterinary practice in the world. Funding came from many sources and for a variety of purposes, one example of which is the Jeanne Marchig International Centre for Animal Welfare Education (JMICAWE).

The buildings combine important modern touches – such as sedum-clad roofs, designed both for fuel economy and to minimise the visual impact of the complex when seen from the adjacent Pentland Hills – with some of the most striking features of the Summerhall building. The stained glass windows from Summerhall, set at an angle above the entrance foyer, can still be appreciated by all who pass through; and William Dick's statue takes pride of place.

The Royal (Dick) School of Veterinary Studies today

The entrance hall of the Dick Vet

## ST CECILIA'S HALL

Completed in 1763, the lovely elliptical upper hall of St Cecilia's was Scotland's first purpose-built concert hall. Situated in the Cowgate and now encased in a largely 1960s outer shell with a somewhat un-prepossessing entrance, it is a little hard to find. The hall fell out of use as a concert hall in 1798, thereafter suffering many changes of use and of ownership before being taken over by the city council. It was then used for a variety of purposes by a range of tenants. In 1959, needing premises for an expanded Faculty of Music, the University purchased the dilapidated hall from the council and began an ambitious pro-gramme of renovation and restoration, opening St Cecilia's in 1968 as a concert venue once more. In the meantime, a very substantial gift had been offered to the University; the English antiquarian and col-lector Raymond Russell (1922–64) offered his magnificent collection of early keyboard instruments, and these are on display in St Cecilia's. Other collections have followed and are covered in Chapter 6.

The University's purchase of St Cecilia's has strengthened links with the city and beyond. Used by the Georgian Concert Society and others for performances, the hall is supported by Friends of St Cecilia's Hall and Museum. The Friends, a charity independent of the University, help the hall in many ways – providing funds for the purchase of instruments for the collections, awarding bursaries for

St Cecilia's Hall

undergraduate and postgraduate research projects and contributing to the fabric of the hall too.

Plans are underway for a major refurbishment of St Cecilia's, thanks to a very generous donation from Dr Joy Sypert and Dr George Sypert. The Syperts are passionate supporters of St Cecilia's Hall and previous donations have enabled the purchase of several important instruments and work to the hall itself. This latest donation, combined with a grant from the Heritage Lottery Fund, will ensure that St Cecilia's is more attractive, welcoming and accessible in the future and that its world-famous collection of musical instruments is preserved and used for future generations.

# 4

## Research and Scholarship

A S A WORLD-RENOWNED research institution, the University counts research projects amongst the most crucial of its activities. Research is diverse and broad, covering all disciplines, and varied in approach – clearly science is quite different from medicine or social sciences or history or philosophy. When General Sir Joseph Straton died in 1841, he left a bequest of £14,157 to the University, 'the yearly interest to be applied towards the promotion and advancement of science'. This generosity represented a substantial increase to the University's income, and coming with relatively few 'strings attached', enabled broad development.

General Sir Joseph Straton

One might think that the gift that will influence research most is to endow a chair in a new area or to fund researchers directly or purchase a piece of equipment. Of course, these are key things which enable the University to develop in new directions. But perhaps more surprisingly, new and renovated buildings can have a positive influence on research, as can scholarships. This chapter focuses on philanthropic support which has enabled the discovery of new knowledge and its development. Sometimes a project is started with a clear aim in mind; on other occasions, research produces unexpected spin-offs – and indeed, some projects fail to achieve their original aims

This early cyclotron or particle accelerator was in use around 1950 and is a precursor to the Large Hadron Collider at CERN in Switzerland, where work on detecting the Higgs-Boson particle was carried out

but reveal different information of value. For all these reasons, having the funding available to experiment and try new lines of enquiry is essential to the development of a research-led university like Edinburgh.

One unexpected outcome which occurred recently has been mentioned above. The renovation of Old College quad and the resultant archaeological dig revealed much more than had been anticipated, and research on the finds will continue for some time to come, adding to our knowledge of the development of Edinburgh as a city, of the University itself and of the scientific discipline of chemistry.

### WORKING IN PARTNERSHIP WITH CHARITIES

The University is a charity in its own right, but often works with funding provided through other charities, as the following examples demonstrate.

*School of Engineering – research into fire safety*

The University has for many years had a large and thriving school of engineering. A very strong research focus across the School has led to the establishment of several world-leading institutes and projects. One of these is the BRE (Building Research Establishment) Centre for Fire Safety Engineering.

For over forty years, the University has been at the forefront of fire safety research and is one of five BRE University Centres of Excellence and the only one in this field in the UK; many of the world's leading fire safety practitioners have studied at Edinburgh at some point. Edinburgh's work is underpinned by the BRE Trust and Ove Arup and Partners Ltd, with the goal of 'building a better world together'.

The BRE Trust is the UK's largest charity dedicated to research and development in the built environment, and commissions research with the aim of achieving a higher-quality built environment, built facilities which offer improved functionality and value for money, and a more efficient and sustainable construction sector with a higher level of innovative practice. The BRE Professorship of Fire Safety Engineering is currently held by Albert Simeoni, who leads the BRE Centre on this work of vital importance in saving lives across the world.

Fire Science at Edinburgh would never have existed without the continuous support of Dr Frank Rushbrook, a former Firemaster of Edinburgh and South-East of Scotland Fire Brigade and an international fire expert, particularly in ship fires. In the early 1970s, he convinced the University to establish the first department for fire engineering in the world. Dr Rushbrook set about raising the funds to support the appointment of a professor and two lecturers. Under the leadership of Professor Rasbash, the team at Edinburgh developed the first postgraduate course in fire safety engineering globally.

Dr Frank Rushbrook with a 'fire tornado'

The curriculum broke new ground and set academic standards for the subject. With the success of the postgraduate programme, Dr Rushbrook helped raise funds to support a third lecturer. In 2001, Dr Rushbrook made a gift to the University to build the Rushbrook Fire Laboratory. This state-of-the-art fire research laboratory is unique to Edinburgh and cemented the research group's position as among the best in the world. This gift played a major role in attracting fellow fire safety visionary Professor José Torero to lead research and teaching on this subject at Edinburgh. In 2012, Dr Rushbrook realised a further vision with a personal donation – to develop research and teaching in fire investigation. The Rushbrook Lectureship in Fire Investigation was established.

In 2013, Luke Bisby was appointed as Arup Professor of Fire Structures, an appointment supported by Ove Arup and Partners Ltd, one of the world's leading built environment design consultancies. The aim of this new appointment is to help move the concept of structural fire engineering from a specialist interest area to a core engineering discipline, fully integrated into the building design process. The support by Ove Arup and Partners Ltd and the Ove Arup Foundation acknowledges the particularity of fire science at the University. The Foundation's mission, with a focus on education promoting new thinking and initiatives likely to reach a wide audience around the world, fits well with the University's own mission.

### Palliative care

The World Health Organization describes palliative care as

> an approach that improves the quality of life of patients and their families facing the problem associated with life-threatening illness, through the prevention and relief of suffering by means of early identification and impeccable assessment and treatment of pain and other problems, physical, psychosocial and spiritual.

The Primary Palliative Care Research Group is a multidisciplinary team based at the University of Edinburgh, though with strong international links. Professor Scott Murray, whose chair was endowed by St Columba's Hospice, leads a team working with general practitioners, community nurses, psychologists, epidemiologists, patient and carer groups, and many others with the shared vision of extending the scope and impact of palliative care locally and internationally. The group is recognised as an international leader in multi-perspective qualitative longitudinal research and is now advocating for a more equitable provision of palliative care. Work was already starting in this area, but the establishment of this first UK Chair of Palliative Care in the Community through the donation from St Columba's Hospice in 2006 really stimulated the work of the group. The group has been at the forefront of efforts to extend palliative care so that it no longer focuses mainly on terminal care of cancer patients in economically developed countries, but seeks to address the needs of people with all advanced illnesses internationally. The funding has allowed the group to research into improved care from an early stage in illness. Collaborative partnerships between the University, NHS researchers and other charities such as Marie Curie Cancer Care and Macmillan Cancer Relief have also been very useful. Publications and policy documents have followed, and the group is now working in the Far East and Africa to integrate palliative care into health services there. The donation from St Columba's Hospice has therefore led to research that has improved services and created visionary policies within Scotland, as well as having an impact overseas.

## Cancer research in Edinburgh

Cancer Research UK is now the major cancer charity in the UK but its forerunner with the Cancer Research Campaign was the Imperial Cancer Research Fund (ICRF). In 1978, ICRF endowed a Chair in Medical Oncology with a donation of £800,000; Professor John Smyth was appointed to that Chair in 1979 and served until 2008. During the late 1990s, as a result of a very successful quinquennial review, ICRF expressed their support for expanding the laboratory programme of cancer research in Edinburgh. Professor Smyth was aware that the existing laboratory accommodation was too small to attract world-class laboratory-based researchers and obtained permission to raise funds for what is now the Cancer Research Building on the Western General Hospital Campus. The above-mentioned endowment had been so well invested that in addition to funding the core members of

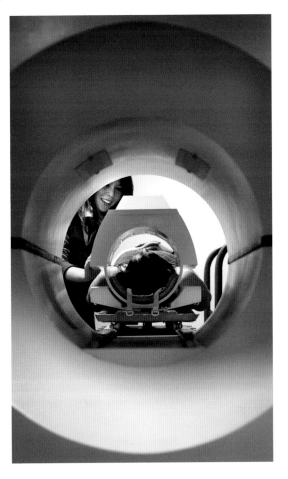

A patient undergoing an MRI scan

University staff, sufficient funds were available for the University to release £5 million towards the Cancer Research Building. Over an eighteen-month period an additional £2 million was raised, primarily from local philanthropists, and the £7 million facility was opened by HRH The Princess Royal in 2002.

Buildings may only be bricks and mortar, but the philanthropy that enabled the construction of this building provided a magnificent facility for the multidisciplinary exchange necessary for contemporary cancer research. The primary purpose was to provide laboratory accommodation, but the facility also housed psychologists, clinicians and the palliative care team to enhance a mutual understanding of the breadth of cancer research being undertaken in Edinburgh. In the decade that followed construction of the Edinburgh Cancer Research Centre, research has expanded considerably and is reflected in the most recent significant enhancement to Cancer Research UK funding to the University.

The view across Princes Street Gardens to New College in the 1860s

The Wode Psalter

### Divinity and the Wode Psalter project

The School of Divinity could arguably make the case for being the University's original *raison d'être*. At the time when the Tounis College was first set up, the main purpose of any university was the training of men for the Church. Robert Reid, Bishop of Orkney, left provision in his will in 1558 for the foundation of a college in Edinburgh to teach the 'new learning', and his bequest formed part of the money used by the town council for the foundation of the Tounis College in 1583. Under close scrutiny from the town council, the Tounis College provided both education in the liberal arts and training for the new (Protestant) ministry. In 1582, a procession of Edinburgh Presbyterians marched up the High Street singing Psalm 124 in four-part harmony. The setting they used came from manuscript 'part-books' created by Thomas Wode (pronounced Wood).

The Kirby Laing Foundation was established in 1972 and supports a wide range of charities in the UK and abroad. For some years, the generosity of the Foundation has

New College in the spring

supported teaching in Reformation history and theology at the University of Edinburgh. Professor Jane Dawson, John Laing Professor of Reformation History, led a research project on the Wode Psalter which culminated in a major exhibition and musical concerts during the Edinburgh International Festival in 2011.

The Wode or St Andrews Psalter comprises manuscript musical settings from the Book of Psalms. Thomas Wode, who was a Catholic monk prior to the Reformation in Scotland, collected harmonisations of the metrical psalms from the 1564 Scottish Psalm Book into part-books, creating the 'gold standard' for post-Reformation devotion and worship in Scotland. Not simply a very important collection of early modern Scottish music, the many illustrations and illuminating marginalia in the Wode Psalter provide valuable insights into post-Reformation Scottish history and culture. This is highly relevant to the University's own history, given that the Tounis College was founded against this very background of religious and political turmoil.

### Oral history – a tradition preserved

The School of History, Classics and Archaeology recently received funding from the Northern Lighthouse Heritage Trust to undertake a fascinating oral history initiative. A large-scale fieldwork project will be carried out, recording the oral testimonies of former lighthouse keepers and their families who have served with the Northern Lighthouse Board in Scotland. The project will be managed by Dr Wendy Ugolini. The collected material will ultimately be deposited in the School of Scottish Studies Archive, University of Edinburgh, for the availability of future researchers.

## MEDICAL RESEARCH, FOR THE BENEFIT OF OTHERS

Some donors are prompted to facilitate research in a specific area, having perhaps experienced within their families the devastation caused by some conditions. Funding research in this way may often come too late to help the individual, but will bring enormous benefit to society in the longer term.

### The Dr Albert S. McKern Fellowship

Dr Albert McKern was from Australia and studied at the University of Sydney and thereafter at Yale University before taking up a place at Edinburgh. He graduated in medicine from Edinburgh shortly after the First World War and practised medicine in Malaya (now Singapore). He died in a Japanese internment camp in Sumatra, but had specified in his will, written in Malaya in 1944, that ten years after the death of his last immediate family member, the proceeds of his estate should be divided between the three universities he had attended. Edinburgh has a leading role in research into pregnancy and childbirth, thanks to the legacy that has established the Dr Albert S. McKern Fellowship.

### The Euan MacDonald Centre for Motor Neurone Disease Research

Motor neurone disease (MND), also called amyotrophic lateral sclerosis (ALS), is a progressive and fatal neurological condition that a multidisciplinary team based at the University is working hard to understand and develop treatment for. Through its research, the Centre aims to make a difference to the lives of people living with MND, and their families.

The Euan MacDonald Centre
for Motor Neurone Disease
Research and the Anne Rowling
Regenerative Neurology Clinic
provide research and clinic facilities

The Euan MacDonald Centre is a 'centre without walls' of thirty researchers who undertake fundamental discovery research combined with a growing portfolio of patient-centred research projects. Anchored at Little France, but with investigators and postgraduate students across Scotland and collaborators worldwide, the Centre is a global leader in efforts to model the condition, including in human stem cells.

The research is closely integrated with a fortnightly multidisciplinary NHS specialist clinic that takes place at the Anne Rowling Regenerative Neurology Clinic. When patients come to the clinic they have access to state-of-the-art facilities and a care team that meets a full spectrum of needs. This includes diagnosis, counselling and support plus advice on symptom management such as ventilation as well as physiotherapy and speech and language therapy.

Importantly, patients attending the MND clinic have access to Euan MacDonald Centre research projects. Examples include the Scottish

Fighting back against
motor neurone disease

*hear my voice*

Voicebanking is one of the Euan
MacDonald Centre's clinical
research initiatives

MND Audit Research and Trials (SMART) Register and DNA bank, the Edinburgh Cognitive ALS Screen and the donation of a skin biopsy from which stem cells can be isolated and grown 'in a dish'. The Voicebank project is an initiative to generate bespoke synthesised voices for use in communication aids. Although still in the development stage, it holds great promise for people with MND and other conditions who are losing the ability to speak.

All this was made possible through the vision of two people and in collaboration with others. In 2003, Euan MacDonald, a University of Edinburgh law graduate, was working in corporate finance. A keen sports enthusiast, he was purchasing a bicycle when he discovered he was unable to move through the gears. It was the first sign of a disease that would slowly degrade his motor nerve cells. In 2007, together with his father Donald MacDonald, Euan made a seven-figure donation to the University to establish the Euan MacDonald Centre for Motor Neurone Disease Research. Nine years after diagnosis, Euan remains closely involved with the strategic development of the Centre in his name.

The MacDonalds' donation has also attracted £3 million of additional investment, which supports the work of six professors, has reanimated the national register for MND and has brought together the work of nearly seventy researchers worldwide. The fight against MND is gathering pace, aided by many donors and supporters.

### The Anne Rowling Regenerative Neurology Clinic

Working very closely with staff from the Euan MacDonald Centre and the Patrick Wild Centre, the Anne Rowling Clinic firmly establishes Edinburgh as a leading centre for regenerative neurology and clinical trials. The Clinic has been made possible by the largest single gift ever made to the University – a donation (with Gift Aid) of £12.8 million from the author J. K. Rowling in memory of her mother, Anne, who died aged forty-five from complications related to multiple sclerosis.

The Anne Rowling Clinic combines many things – a clinic for patients, a world-leading research centre and a research training facility for clinical scientists. The building itself provides a calm and welcoming atmosphere, with seven well-equipped consulting rooms, a quiet

The Anne Rowling Regenerative Neurology Clinic

Author J. K. Rowling buried a time capsule prior to the building of the Clinic which bears her mother's name

room and a soundproof room for voice-banking. It has been designed thoughtfully and is filled with natural light. An ongoing collaboration with Edinburgh College of Art provides works which enhance the space and enrich the experience of patients. As J. K. Rowling has said:

> Quite apart from the fantastic staff who have been assembled from around the globe to run the Clinic, I am also very impressed with the building itself. It is humbling to see the plans so quickly translated into a living, functioning centre where clinicians, researchers and, most importantly, patients can find their needs met. Every detail seems to have been considered, and I love how the design and the quality of light create a relaxed, unintimidating and comfortable space where people with these conditions would like to spend time.

Sixty clinics are held each month, covering multiple sclerosis, motor neurone disease, cognitive disorders, movement disorders, brain haemorrhage after stroke, autism and Huntington's disease. In its first year of operation,

2,500 patients were seen, and feedback has been enormously posi-tive, with a strong feeling of involvement and patient engagement through various media, including biannual newsletters, patient information evenings, websites and social media. Patient-scientist question-and-answer sessions allow scientists to interact with people with these diseases, and give more meaning to the scientists' research.

A vision to integrate research with clinics facilitates the transla-tion of research findings into benefits for patients. The clinic's physi-cal location aids collaboration with other research centres, including the MRC Centre for Regenerative Medicine, the Queen's Medical Research Institute, the BioQuarter, the Edinburgh Clinical Research Facility and the Clinical Research Imaging Centre. The Rowling Scholarships advance the next generation of clinical scientists by pro-viding funding for PhD study, providing the essential link between research and clinical practice, 'from bench to bedside research'.

## HONOURING A MEMORY

In establishing a research activity, some donors seek to honour the memory of someone who themselves contributed to a discipline in a major way, as the following examples demonstrate.

### The Gardner Bequest – Nursing Studies

The University's Department of Nursing Studies was established in 1956 and was the first academic department of nursing in Europe. Mr William H. Gardner donated and subsequently bequeathed a fund to support the work and aspirations of Nursing Studies in memory of his late wife, Elsie Stephenson, who had been the first Director of Nursing Studies.

The fund was set up in 1978 to support nursing research, research fellowships and activities which further the knowledge and practice of nursing. The bequest supports Nursing Studies in the public en-gagement of nursing and nursing scholarship through lectures and conferences. It also supports the advancement of nursing knowledge through research. A number of Gardner Scholarships have been awarded to enable nursing graduates from the University of Edin-burgh to undertake doctoral studies; four Gardner Scholars are fea-tured below.

Victoria Traynor is now Associate Professor and Director of the New South Wales (NSW) and Australian Capital Territory (ACT) Australia Dementia Training and Study Centre. The Centre's work complements the aged and dementia care research and education activities which Dr Traynor leads with industry and academic partners across Australia.

Lynn Calman completed a PhD on patients' views of nurses' competence: a grounded theory approach. She has since worked as a research fellow at the University of Manchester where she undertook research on lung cancer patients' priority information needs and preferred level of involvement in treatment and decision-making. Dr Calman is now Senior Research Fellow in the Macmillan Survivorship Research Group (MSRG) in the Faculty of Health Sciences at the University of Southampton. The team work closely with people affected by cancer as research partners in the development and conduct of research projects.

Two recent Gardner Scholars, Sarah Rhynas and Rosie Stenhouse, are now teaching and researching in Nursing Studies at the University. Dr Rhynas' doctoral study explored nurses' conceptualisation of dementia and how these conceptualisations shape nursing practice. Her research interests include the use of dementia care strategies to support alcohol-related brain-damaged (ARBD) patients, innovative approaches to data collection with this group and long-term service development. Dr Rhynas has been involved in a project to compare older people's voices across three decades by analysing archive video material and recent digital recordings of the 'oldest old' to challenge traditional stereotypes of ageing.

Dr Stenhouse's PhD study focused on the experience of being a patient on an acute psychiatric ward, using narrative methods. The narratives were then analysed and transformed into poetic form and have been used as a means of teaching students and engaging wider audiences with the experience of being a psychiatric patient. In another project she used digital storytelling to gather and present the stories of people with dementia. The stories were then collated with reflective questions and developed into an e-learning package to engage students emotionally and cognitively with service users' experiences: 'to put compassion back at the heart of social care'.

As these four Gardner Scholars illustrate, the Gardner Bequest supports nursing graduates from the University of Edinburgh to develop their academic careers and create opportunities to become leaders in their specialist fields. Each one of them has made a significant contribution to nursing research and evidence which supports students' learning and practitioners to make a difference to the quality of patients' care. Their work also makes visible the significance of nursing research to scholarship and practice by creating a living legacy to the first Director of Nursing Studies, Elsie Stephenson, in whose memory the Bequest was established.

### *The Watson Gordon Chair of Fine Art*

The Watson Gordon Chair of Fine Art is named after Sir John Watson Gordon (1788–1864), one of Britain's leading portrait painters and President of the Royal Scottish Academy. To commemorate Sir John's distinguished career, his brother George Henry Watson and sister Miss Frances Watson proposed to the University of Edinburgh that a Chair of Fine Art be established in his name, and their endowment of £11,000 was accepted by the University Court on 30 October 1872. The full sum was only received on the death of Henry Watson in 1879, and the first appointment to the Chair, Gerard Baldwin Brown, was appointed in 1880. The Regulations for the Management of the Chair required the Watson Gordon Professor to provide 'a continuous course of instruction occupying at least twenty weeks of each winter session', and that 'the lectures shall not be fewer than forty'. In 1947, the five-year fine art degree, jointly taught with Edinburgh College of Art, was established.

In 2005, the 125th anniversary of the founding of the Watson Gordon Chair of Fine Art was celebrated with lectures given by four distinguished writers on art, the academics Ludmilla Jordanova, T. J. Clark and Paul Binski, and the art critic Richard Cork. This programme was supported from a bequest of £47,000 from alumna Ann Powell, the main amount of which has been invested in postgraduate scholarships and an endowment for student prizes. The success of this short series of lectures led to the establishment in 2006 of an annual Watson Gordon Lecture, for which a benefaction of some £4,000 per annum over ten years is provided by Robert Robertson, son of a former holder of the Chair. Each annual Watson Gordon Lecture is published after the event by National Galleries of Scotland Publications. These prestigious lectures thus present research to a wide audience beyond the University.

### ENTERPRISE AND NEW DIRECTIONS

#### *The Edinburgh Centre for Carbon Innovation*

The Edinburgh Centre for Carbon Innovation (ECCI) now sits in a refurbished school building at the High School Yards site. This innovative project builds on best practice around the world to enable leaders in low carbon to come together to deliver a low-carbon future. It is a partnership with Heriot-Watt University and Edinburgh Napier University and is having a real impact in the sector by enhancing business enterprise and innovation, delivering staff training for what is essentially a new way of working and supporting the implementation of government policy. The unique enterprise for the University was only possible because of a significant donation from an alumnus, George David. His foresight, commitment and engagement with the project in terms of what the Centre will deliver – and the building itself – was crucial. Given the purpose of the Centre, it was crucial that the building to house it should be of the highest environmental building standards. ECCI is housed in the first retrofitted Georgian building in Scotland to receive BREEAM 'Outstanding' certification; BREEAM sets the standard for best practice in sustainable design and has become the measure used to describe the environmental performance of buildings and communities. ECCI, working on sustainability, thus operates in a building which reflects the whole purpose of the centre.

The Edinburgh Centre for Carbon Innovation in High School Yards

One of the key ambitions of the University is to engage much more with policy makers to ensure research is used to develop evidence-based policy. The Centre is already beginning to lead the agenda on carbon innovation and climate change, linking researchers to the policy makers.

The Centre works with experts, opinion formers and community representatives to explore our energy future and involve the wider public. It is fantastic that a philanthropic gift from someone so committed to sustainable solutions in business enabled this innovative approach to a real-world problem to be established with a stunning space which encourages dialogue and collaboration.

### Noreen and Kenneth Murray

Philanthropists Professor Sir Kenneth Murray and Professor Lady Noreen Murray have been instrumental in changing research direction and ensuring biology research remains world-leading at the University of Edinburgh. Their own research into recombinant DNA technology was innovative and changed technology for ever, enabling a whole new field of molecular genetics and gene cloning to grow. It was as part of this research that Ken Murray developed a hepatitis vaccine that has saved millions of lives. Instead of enjoying a wealthy lifestyle, they both continued to work in their laboratories until their deaths and to give their money to help others. They set up the Darwin Trust, named after Charles Darwin, who arrived in Edinburgh in 1825 to study medicine but turned his attentions to biology, leaving Edinburgh in 1827 without graduating. The Darwin Trust ensures that large numbers of PhD students from other countries can come to Edinburgh to do research in a variety of areas, each contributing to the research of the School of Biology, as well as enabling them to establish their own careers. Donated funding was used to purchase essential equipment for the Biocomputing Research Unit; in turn this enabled structural biology to come to the Swann Building (which the Murrays also helped fund). The close cooperation of structural biologists with biotechnology has led to significant research developments. More recently, the Darwin Trust gave support for cryo-electron microscopy. The availability of this state-of-the-art equipment has enabled many new research directions in cell biology as well as molecular biology, genetics and developmental biology. In addition to considerable generosity during his lifetime, Ken Murray bequeathed £200,000 for research in biological sciences at Edinburgh when he died in 2013, as

Darwin's interests lay in biology rather than medicine

Kenneth and Noreen Murray, painted in the Darwin Building, King's Buildings, by Fionna Carlisle in 2009

well as bequests to other universities and institutions. The bulk of the Murrays' estate was left to the Darwin Trust which will continue to support PhD scholarships in biology.

### The development of a discipline

Geography at Edinburgh celebrated its official centenary in 2008. George Goudie Chisholm was appointed in 1907 to start teaching the subject from the beginning of the following academic year, though in fact 'chorographie' or regional study had been a subject taught by the University's first Principal, Robert Rollock, from the foundation of the University in 1583. The teaching of geography was included as part of philosophy from the 1620s – in particular in relation to 'cosmography' – and, in the 1740s, geography was taught within the mathematics curriculum by the leading Newtonian Colin MacLaurin. James Pillans, professor of humanity from 1820 to 1863, included teaching in geography as part of his classes in ancient history. In its concerns

John Bartholomew & Son Ltd pioneered map design and production

with human-environment relationships, geography is a subject which embraces the 'sciences' and the 'arts' with equal facility. Geography at Edinburgh today (now within the School of Geosciences) is a strong and vital subject incorporating human geography (the humanities and the social sciences) and physical geography (the Earth's surface processes and the natural sciences).

The discipline has benefited from numerous distinguished Edinburgh graduates. One name will be familiar to anyone who has either picked up an atlas or looked at a road map.

John (Ian) Bartholomew (1890–1962) was the fourth in a line of six Bartholomews to be involved in cartography; his great-great-grandfather George worked with the Edinburgh engraver Daniel Lizars in the late eighteenth century. Under a series of descendants, all named John, Bartholomew and Son Ltd. became the pre-eminent publisher of maps and atlases in Britain and carried the title 'Geographers and Cartographers Royal', working from 1910 onwards from the Edinburgh Geographical Institute which they founded. John (Ian) Bartholomew studied cartography at Edinburgh, Leipzig and Paris. His firm pioneered the map design and production mechanisms which led to the *Times Survey Atlas of the World* (1922); John supported the geography department with library materials and well-equipped laboratories and, with support from the Royal Scottish Geographical Society, helped fund the appointment of Edinburgh's first professor of geography, Alan Grant Ogilvie, in 1931. Bartholomew's support of his *alma mater* in this way was a fitting tribute from someone whose family firm had been at the cutting edge of research in its field.

To mark the centenary of geography at Edinburgh, two research endowment funds were established to support postgraduate students in geography, one through the donations of globally based alumni, and the other through the Edinburgh University Club of Toronto. To date, over fifteen PhD students have benefited from this support. A one-off research fund was generously provided by Mr Derek Moss and Mrs Maureen Moss, specifically to assist younger scholars with their research. The range of the projects covered by the three recipients – on the geography and history of evangelical religion in early twentieth-century Peru, towards a book on 'fighting gentrification' and on understanding the social experience of noise from wind farms – is indicative of the depth and the broad reach of the subject in and beyond the University today.

SIMPLE CURIOSITY – FOLLOWING AN INTEREST

A tendency in recent years to focus on results and 'value for money' sometimes suggests that there is no longer any scope to research a topic out of simple curiosity – the so-called 'blue skies' research which nevertheless often turns up results of enormous value to society. Some remarkable benefactors, spurred on primarily by their own curiosity, have enabled some fascinating work to go ahead.

### The Scottish Centre for Diaspora Studies

The University's global reach is arguably part of the disproportionate influence that Scots have historically had on the world. So many major inventions and developments – in science, medicine and industry – have been initiated by natives of this small country. And yet, almost from its foundation, the University has attracted students from abroad too.

Edinburgh alumnus Alan McFarlane was intrigued to note, on his extensive travels on business, that every Australian town seemed to boast a statue of Robert Burns. With his curiosity roused, Mr McFarlane came across the work of Professor Tom Devine on the Scottish diaspora, and he made a very significant donation in 2007 to aid the establishment of the Scottish Centre for Diaspora Studies. With his wife, Anne, also a graduate of Edinburgh, Mr McFarlane was keen to establish scholarships to enable research into the history of Scottish emigration, the impact of Scottish mobility on countries abroad and related themes.

Whilst Scotland will always remain a core area of interest for the Centre, as its work matures increasing attention is being given to comparative studies, generic diaspora themes and the migration histories of other ethnicities, all of which are subjects of current political, social, economic and cultural relevance.

### General William Tweedie

William Tweedie joined the Honorable East India Company's Army in 1857 as a twenty-one-year-old cadet. Rising rapidly through the ranks, he spent the majority of his career in India, with forays into Afghanistan and the Middle East. An authority on the Arabian horse, on which he wrote extensively, he retired to Scotland in 1902. In 1913, he drew up directions for the trust which bears his name and which is managed by the University.

The Tweedie Exploration Fund gives small grants to research students and recent graduates, not necessarily of the University of Edinburgh, for ethnological (including archaeological), sociological or linguistic research in lesser-known regions of the world. Tweedie was quite specific about both the type of scholar and the type of research he wished to support. Whilst the committee no longer considers whether the 'young scholars [are] of practically sound mind and body', preference is still given to research in the areas which most interested Tweedie – 'philosophic investigation ... in Asia or in Africa of all above-ground traces or vestiges lying latent in religion, language, physical characteristics, opinions, beliefs, customs, laws and institutions generally as well as in ancient writings and inscriptions...'

```
.....The University authorities shall faithfully guard against even the smallest
portion of these Trust Funds being expended on extraneous objects, such as
archaeological excavation, the creation of library wings or adjuncts, payment
to librarians; Lectureships, whether permanently endowed as e.g. "readerships"
auxiliary to Oriental Language Professorships in the Scottish Universities;  or
more special like the "Gifford Lectures" with their tendency to drift towards
"Emeritus" Professors; or on outfits or on compensation to stipendiaries or
their relations; or on grants for the printing or the translating of the copying
of books or MSS.; or on office rents, allowances to servitors, petty officials
or the like; and last but not least against the appointment of amateur, dilett-
ante or desultory applicants whose objects, when sifted, would appear to be
proper to themselves, such as to see the world; write a book; obtain a change
of climate, and so on.
```

In entrusting the University with this task, Tweedie explained that 'My desire is ... to leave my substance for the sending forth of men better qualified than I ever was to bring forth distinctive results in the special field or fields ... of Comparative Sociology and Anthropology in the fullest and widest sense'.

Tweedie specified how he wished his funds to be spent – and how they should not be spent

### Building on the work of an early Principal

William Robertson (1721–93), who became Principal of the University in 1762 and Historiographer Royal in 1764, was a leading scholar of the Scottish Enlightenment. By profession a Church of Scotland minister, Robertson was a pioneer of historical studies at a time when history was not yet a distinct subject. His writings *History of Scotland*

*during the Reigns of Queen Mary and James VI* (1759), together with histories of America and of the Emperor Charles V, were some of the most influential historical works of the eighteenth century.

Archaeology too started as an amateur pursuit for many. The teaching of Latin was, of course, of vital importance in the early years of the University, and the School of History, Classics and Archaeology now covers the three disciplines. Archaeology in various guises has been taught within the University of Edinburgh since the nineteenth century, but the establishment of the modern department, focused principally on prehistoric archaeology, began almost a century ago. Dr Robert Munro (1835–1920) was a distinguished amateur archaeologist best known for his books on lake dwellings.

Munro inaugurated a lecture series in prehistoric archaeology and anthropology. He delivered the initial series of Munro Lectures

John Kay's portrait of the Historiographer Royal, William Robertson

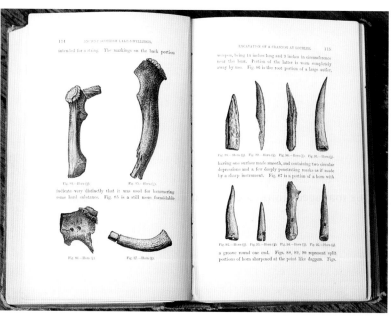

Dr Robert Munro researched and wrote extensively on the Scottish lake dwellings

himself, and he published them in 1912 as 'Palaeolithic man and terramara settlements in Europe'. The Munro Lectures continue on an annual basis, bringing together a wide range of scholars and students.

Also in 1912, another Fellow of the Society of Antiquaries of Scotland, the Hon. John Abercromby (1841–1924), produced his two-volume 'A Study of the Bronze Age Pottery of Great Britain and Ireland', which is widely credited with bringing order to the study of Bronze Age pottery and associated grave-goods. Four years later, and by then Lord Abercromby of Tullibody and Aboukir, he endowed a Chair of Prehistoric Archaeology at the University under the terms of his will. Following his death, the post was advertised and the first incumbent was the Australian archaeologist Vere Gordon Childe (1892–1957). Edinburgh was thus amongst the first universities in Britain to teach archaeology.

Lord Abercromby endowed a Chair of Prehistoric Archaeology

Vere Gordon Childe, the first holder of the Abercromby Chair, seen here in 1957 following the award of the honorary degree of Doctor of Letters from the University of Sydney

Arguably the most distinguished prehistorian of his time, Childe did much of his most significant work during his Edinburgh years, the longest spell he held any academic post. He published a string of important syntheses and academic papers, and is credited with laying the theoretical and methodological foundations of Old World archaeology.

Childe confronted the big issues of the human past, exploring such momentous developments as the origins of agriculture, the rise of complex societies and the emergence of cities; themes which are central to archaeological study at Edinburgh today. A prolific writer, Childe managed simultaneously to develop his international knowledge and contacts whilst also conducting fieldwork in Scotland, where all his most significant excavations took place. The most famous of these was at the Neolithic village of Skara Brae on Orkney, but this project (in which the archaeological component

was largely undertaken by Ministry of Works labourers in preparation for the stabilisation of the site) was atypical of his involvement in field archaeology. Much more of his excavation was carried out in association with his students at a variety of sites including chambered cairns, stone circles and hill-forts.

Classics too benefits from the vision of an enthusiast. Anastasios George Leventis was a Cypriot businessman who made provision in his will for the establishment of a foundation to support educational, artistic, cultural and philanthropic causes in Cyprus, Greece and elsewhere. In 1997, the A. G. Leventis Foundation endowed a chair for a biennial Visiting Research Professorship in Classical Greek to be based in Classics at Edinburgh. The purpose of the Chair is to contribute to the understanding of classical Greece and its literature, history and people. One of the main responsibilities of the professor, while in residence, is to arrange a conference resulting in publication. Eight Leventis conferences have been held at Edinburgh so far, bringing scholars from around the world to share information and research.

### FUTURE DIRECTIONS

As the brief case studies above demonstrate, research is carried out for a wide variety of reasons, the funding strands are many and varied, and research may have an impact very locally or individually, or on a global scale.

The freedom to follow their interests and discover new things is one of the main reasons people choose to become academics. Staff of the University of Edinburgh – individually and as part of research teams - are very successful in bidding for research funding from the national research councils, from government bodies and from international sources, but without charity and philanthropic funding, many new discoveries would never have been made. Research requires not just imagination, ideas and crucial skills, but time and equipment, and access to materials. All this comes at a considerable cost, and the support of donors is a vital component in the development of research.

# 5

## Bursaries, Scholarships and Prizes

G AINING A UNIVERSITY EDUCATION has always represented a commitment of time and effort, and has usually en-
tailed a heavy financial commitment too. For many people,
this has been a barrier to education, but it is evident that from the
very earliest days of the University, benefactors were keen to do what
they could to enable suitably qualified students to study, regardless of
their financial background.

### TYPES OF STUDENT FINANCIAL SUPPORT

Funding for students now tends to be categorised as 'bursaries', 'prizes'
or 'scholarships', and though those labels have not been consistently
applied in the past, it is worth giving some modern definitions.

Bursaries are usually based on financial need coupled with eligibility criteria; a bursary may fund or part-fund a student for all or
part of the duration of their studies. Scholarships are usually awarded
on academic or sporting merit, and are usually competitive; again,
a scholarship may provide full or part-funding for a student. Prizes
are normally competitive one-off awards, of relatively low financial
value when compared with scholarships or bursaries, but of enormous importance to the recipient. A condition of many bursaries and
scholarships is that recipients make good academic progress.

Delving into minute books, it is clear that some bursaries and
prizes were available from an early point in the University's history.
The creation of scholarships is a more recent innovation.

Thomas Aquilina received an Access Bursary and has since travelled through Africa furthering his work

Thomas Aquilina was a recent recipient of an Access Bursary, and talks here about the difference it has made to him, and his contribution to society:

I was thrilled to graduate in Architecture from the University of Edinburgh last summer [2012] with first-class honours. As the first in my family to attend university and recipient of an Access Bursary, it allowed me to demonstrate as misguided the suggestion that someone from my modest background should not succeed at an elite university. Importantly, the University ensured no complacency on my part, raised ambitions and set goals that would have otherwise been out of reach.

Simply, without the Access Bursary, I might otherwise not have had the opportunity of a university education.

Beyond my degree, I am the RIBA Norman Foster Travelling Scholar. This globally prestigious scholarship is awarded to one student to fund international research on a topic and in a location of their choice. Over the past seven months I have travelled vertically through Africa to six cities (Cairo, Addis Ababa, Kampala, Kigali, Lusaka and Johannesburg), documenting informal livelihoods and recycled architecture. I travelled consciously, keeping in mind the attitudes that served me well as an undergraduate: persistence, curiosity and thirst for knowledge.

Thomas is in a long line of deserving students who have been helped financially over the past 430 years; the need for support for students was recognised even before the foundation of the University. The Reformation of 1560 created a number of acts that shaped the daily lives of the Scottish people. *The First Book of Discipline*, commissioned by the Church of Scotland, had a profound impact on education in Scotland. John Knox was one member of the commission that authored this

'Saturated People' – Kampala, Uganda: photograph by Thomas Aquilina, 2013

text, and in a chapter entitled 'The Necessity of Schools', he spoke of the vital role of communities in supporting the education of their most promising students:

> The children of the poor must be supported and sustained on the charge of the Church, till trial be taken whether the spirit of docility be found in them or not. If they be found apt to letters and learning then may they not,—we mean, neither the sons of the rich, nor yet the sons of the poor,—be permitted to reject learning, but must be charged to continue their study, so that the commonwealth may have some comfort by them.

Knox's vision anticipated the benefits to society of broadening access to education. His appeal to the parish appears to have been successful, though records are scant. This early form of bursary enabled many boys to complete an education, with the local 'dominie' (schoolmaster) selecting the most deserving boys and sourcing funding to enable them to continue to university.

IOANNES CNOXVS.

John Knox in c. 1580

## EARLY BURSARIES AND ADMINISTRATIVE DIFFICULTIES

Donors have often sought to specify criteria for the use of their funds. Whilst this is understandable, it can on occasion make it difficult to put the funds to best use. Donors these days are encouraged to attach as few strings as possible, thereby enabling the University to award funding on the basis of current demographics and where it is most needed. In the early days of the University, donors might restrict funds to those bearing a particular name, coming from a certain town or having been educated at a specified school.

The Stewart Bursary was established in 1810, the total fund being £603. This was to be used for three bursaries, to be given each year for three years, open to second-year students and following a 'trial' in which applicants had to translate English into Latin and Latin into

Sir John Macpherson, as depicted by William Cuming

English, be examined in Greek and translate Greek to English. The Stewart Bursary was one of a number of bursaries intended only for those with specific surnames, though one famous Stewart bursar, of whom more later, benefited from the possibility of a recipient also bearing the surname 'Simpson'. Another name-specific bursary was the Grant Bursary, open to 'those young men to be of the name of Grant', established in 1826 by Donald Grant.

Other bursaries had different eligibility requirements. The Senatus noted in February 1821 that Sir John Macpherson (a previous acting Governor-General of India and an alumnus of Edinburgh) 'bequeathed £2000 … to provide an Annual Bursary to any Highland Student who understands the nature of Gaelic and may be selected by the Professors for said Bursary'.

Keeping track of donations to the University has not always been an easy task. Fleeting references to bursaries and scholarships in the early history of the University do exist, but there are no reliable records before the Senatus Academicus started to maintain them in the 1730s. The first concrete mention of bursaries is on 28 May 1735, when Laurence Dundas, professor of humanity, 'mortifies' (a Scots legal term relating to a bequest to a charity) three bursaries of £100 (Scots) yearly:

> For maintaining and educating three bursars at the Philosophy College … for the space of five years with the express provision that the said Bursars shall each of them be oblidged to spend and employ the first two years of the five … in said College.

In 1751, the minutes noted that 'it is enjoined to the Principal Professor of Humanity in terms of the mortification to examine the said Bursars if they are fit to go forward in their studies'.

For both scholarships and bursaries, reviews of the student's progress may be necessary to ensure the student is still eligible for the funding – through above average performance, continuing financial need or simply proof of attendance at classes. It is clear that this has not always been straightforward. On 7 December 1778 the Senatus Academicus noted that

> Altho it is known that there are about forty Bursaries belonging to the classes of the above named professors [Ferguson, Bruce, Hill, Dalziel, Dugald Stewart and John Robison], they have not been applied to for twenty Certificates of Attendance for these two years past, and at all times the applications for this purpose have not amounted to one fourth of those which should have been made … They have therefore the greatest reason to believe that great Abuses are committed in this respect to the frustration of the kind intentions of the donors and the hurt of this University.

Delays in payments of bursary funds from the executors of benefactors' wills were relatively common. Establishment of the Short Bursary was noted on 8 December 1777, with a caveat:

> Mr James Short of London had by last will bequeathed two hundred pounds to the University to be applied for establishing a Mathematical Bursary … it appeared that the Executor had some difficulty with respect to payment of the said fund.

In July 1778, the minutes noted that 'there was now a prospect of a speedy pay' provided arrangements were made for a power of attorney. The University promptly made the necessary authorisations, but did not receive the money until 31 January 1794.

Lack of information available to staff and students about bursaries sometimes meant they were not used for many years. Both the Stewart and Macpherson Bursaries remained vacant and were divided into smaller amounts in November 1845; they were still vacant three years later. On 31 March 1849, it was noted that only three potential Stewart Bursars appeared for the exams 'and … the Examination in Classics passed by these three, was so indifferent, that the Faculty cannot recommend the Senatus to confer the Bursary on any of them'. On 23 February 1850, the Stewart Bursary remained without competitors, let alone a recipient.

Record-keeping on funds held, partly inherited from the town council, was fairly sporadic. Apparently frustrated with this, on 31 January 1794 the Senatus Academicus made the first of several requests that 'an exact amount should, if possible, be procured of all the Bursaries [to be] laid before the Senatus Academicus'. That request led to the establishment of the Bursary Committee, designed to gather and maintain records of student bursaries. In November 1821

> The Committee agreed to recommend to the Senatus that applications be renewed to the Honourable Patrons for a correct list of the Bursaries which may be held by Students in this University, of the faculties to which such Bursaries are restricted, and of the individuals by whom they are at present drawn.

Despite this recommendation, an absence of reports from the committee until the middle of the 1800s means that little information is available. In October 1841, the Bursary Committee recorded that the 'Principal stated as Convenor of the Committee on Bursaries that matters were not yet ripe for a general report'.

In 1848, a list of sorts was made available, dividing bursaries into two sections – those 'the funds whereof were in the hands of the Town Council' and 'bursaries the funds for which are under management of the Senatus or other parties'. Senatus would have to wait another twenty years before a full list of funds was presented to it.

### PRIZE FUNDS

Whilst the criteria for bursaries are often wide, prize funds can be very narrowly focused, sometimes making it difficult to award them. The expansion of the British Empire brought some fusions of ideology and academic study. In the meeting of the Senatus on 11 June 1804, a letter from Claud Buchanan of Calcutta was discussed, proposing prizes for an essay and a poem (£100 and £60 respectively) as follows:

> 1. An English Dissertation – on the best means of civilising the Subject of the British Empire in India, and of diffusing the light of the Christian Religion throughout the Eastern World.
> 2. An English Poem – On the Restoration of Learning in the East.

The prizes would be paid 'on delivery to Messrs. Boehm & Co. of five copies of Each Work respectively, for the college of Fort William in Bengal'. 'The Senatus Academicus after deliberation, resolved to comply with Mr Buchanan's proposals' and advertised the prizes. A large volume of entries resulted in a longer judging period with the prize essay not selected until 18 February 1807.

In 1846, a student essay was nominated for the Hope Prize in Chemistry, but the view of the judging professors was scathing: 'We regret that, where the intention is excellent, the execution of the Author's purpose should be so defective, as to make it impossible to recommend'. The Hope Prize then remained unclaimed for a further three years as the professor of chemistry was unaware of its existence.

Despite the difficulties in awarding them, the professors recognised the importance of the annual distribution of prizes, noting in 1822

> the great benefit of the measure, by the vigorous exertions to which it prompted their students, by the opportunity which it afforded the deserving of publicly displaying their talents and acquirements; and by the general spirit of attention and industry which it served to awaken and having considered also the deliberate opinion of those professors [whose classes were granted an allowance for prizes], that similar benefits are not to be expected from any other mode of dispensing prizes, than out of a public grant to be scrupulously awarded according to the claim of merit.

## VICTORIAN DEVELOPMENTS
## AND THE RISE OF THE SCHOLARSHIP

Clerk Ranken won the Hope Prize in Chemistry; he graduated BSc in 1902 and DSc in 1907

Robert D. Anderson, Michael Lynch and Nicholas Phillipson, in *The University of Edinburgh: An Illustrated History*, noted the variety of backgrounds from which Edinburgh's students hailed, and that bursaries were vital:

> An official survey of the 1860s tells us the fathers' occupations of two samples of arts students. Roughly 35 per cent came from professional families (such as ministers, doctors and lawyers), 15 per cent from the richer business class, and 15 per cent from farming. But about 8 per cent were drawn from shopkeeping or white-collar families, and 25 per cent from the working-class – though most of the 'working class' fathers were skilled craftsmen rather than labourers, miners or factory workers. These

figures show that, as one might expect, the student body was predominantly middle class, yet also that in Scotland the relatively low fees and living expenses, and the availability of many charitable bursaries, put a university education, and thus entrance into the professions, within reach of a wide social range.

Two important developments in Victorian times put the University onto a much sounder footing than hitherto, and this enabled the rise of a new type of student funding. The Universities (Scotland) Act 1858 increased government funding to universities significantly. And at Edinburgh, a group led by Dr John Muir (1810–82) established the Association for the Better Endowment of the University of Edinburgh in 1864.

D. B. Horn, in *A Short History of the University of Edinburgh 1556–1889* (1967), noted that it was 'characteristic of the Victorian age of self-help that the major contributions to solving the University's cumulative financial problems came in the next generation from generous private benefactions and a substantial growth of income from fees for tuition and graduation'. Nationally, of course, there is evidence of extensive philanthropic giving at that time, with many towns and cities boasting schools, libraries, hospitals and parks founded by local benefactors, but the University was particularly lucky in having Muir's involvement. Grant described Muir as 'the most important of the early benefactors' and 'one of the best friends the University ever had'. Muir was

> celebrated for his knowledge of Sanskrit, and in 1854 retired from the Indian Civil Service to devote his life to study and to the promotion of higher learning and of scientific theology. He was very generous and philanthropical. He not only founded the Sanskrit Chair, but also provided a course of lectures on the Science of Religion, which were delivered 1880–1882 by the Rev. Principal Fairbairn. He was author of an important work in five volumes, entitled *Ancient Sanskrit Texts*. Also of a number of *Metrical Translations from the Sanskrit*.

With the introduction of scholarships – awarded on merit rather than on financial need – a third strand of student funding became available in the nineteenth century.

### THE FIRST SCHOLARSHIPS

In his *The Story of the University of Edinburgh* (1884), Sir Alexander Grant noted the announcement of the Ferguson Scholarships in 1861, which were 'open annually, one in Classics, one in Mathematics, and one in Mental Science, to the students of the four Universities' and which sought 'to reward high attainment in those who had completed their University course'. The Ferguson Scholarships were only of £80 a year for two years, but as Grant explains

> [n]othing was more wanted than something of this kind, as no such encouragement for the higher learning previously existed in Scotland … a Ferguson Scholarship is the 'blue ribbon' for its own department in Scotland, and almost all Ferguson Scholars have turned out distinguished men.

Over the years several philosophers at Edinburgh were awarded the Ferguson Scholarship, including Richard Burdon Haldane (1876), James Seth (1882), Sir William Macdonald (1887), Sir James Black Baillie (1904) and Alan James Dorward (1910). Grant asserted the significance of this first scholarship, explaining that

> [d]own to the date of the foundation of the Ferguson Scholarships (1861), all benefactions for Students had been in the shape of bursaries to help them to get through their course whether well or ill. But now there came a series of rewards provided for those who at the end of their course could show distinction above their fellows.

A. L. Turner also spoke highly of scholarships awarded in recognition of academic achievements, which 'thus serve the vitally important purpose of enabling specially distinguished students, at the critical epoch after graduation, to devote themselves for a further period to strictly academic study'.

The association founded by Muir was particularly useful in publicising the needs of the University, and so garnered considerable public and private support. It could be seen as an extension of the work of Knox and the early parish dominies, as well as a forerunner to the current initiatives driving the unprecedented success of the University's Edinburgh Campaign. Grant explains that the association

Sir Alexander Grant, as painted by
Sir William Llewellyn

has collected funds, not of any great amount, with which it has from time to time provided certain useful scholarships and bursaries, but its chief function has been to make known by annual meetings and reports the wants of the University, and thus to aid in enlisting the sympathy of the public.

The efforts of the Association, no doubt combined with many concurrent causes, and following up the interest which surrounded University of Edinburgh in the commencement of its new life, resulted in the most extraordinary efflorescence of gifts, of a kind which was most wanted, namely, encouragements for the higher learning in Students.'

Over the next twenty years, students were able to compete for an increasing number of scholarships following the influx of funding after the Act of 1858 and the establishment of the Association. In the Faculty of Arts, Grant noted eleven new scholarships, stressing that 'up to 1861 there was absolutely no pecuniary encouragement for Arts Students in the University of Edinburgh to endeavour to distinguish themselves'. Horn reported that

[a]t Edinburgh in less than twenty years, sixteen such scholarships were established in the Arts Faculty, six scholarships or prizes in what would now be called the Faculty of Science, a similar number, though of less emolument, in Divinity and Medicine, and two in Law

and so 'by the 1880s the University for the first time possessed the means to encourage the best of its graduates to proceed to further study and research'.

### PATRONS AND BENEFACTORS – AND RECIPIENTS

With a large number of donors over the years, choosing only a couple of case studies is difficult. The three examples below have been selected for the impact just some of their recipients have made.

*Dr Andrew Vans Dunlop*

One notable benefactor was Dr Andrew Vans Dunlop (1805–80), who had been a surgeon for the East India Company in the Bengal Medical Service. Aside from a few mentions in *The Asiatic Journal* (May–August 1836) of his moves through India as an assistant surgeon, it is difficult to find any other information about him, but after his retirement he lived in Edinburgh and was a member of a committee which produced a report in 1868 entitled 'The Condition of the Poorer Classes of Edinburgh and of their Dwellings, Neighbourhoods, and Families'. Details of his bequest were published in *The British Medical Journal* on 20 March 1880, very soon after his death:

Dr Andrew Vans Dunlop, by John Henry Lorimer

> The University of Edinburgh has just been made the subject of a munificent bequest by the late Dr. Andrew Vans Dunlop, of 18, Rutland Square, Edinburgh. He has left it the residue of his estate, amounting to about £50,000. Of this sum, £30,000 will, it is understood, be paid to the University authorities; while the remaining £20,000, which is life-rented by a relative of Dr. Dunlop, will ultimately accrue to the University. With regard to the purpose for which the money is left, there is instruction in the will that £3,000 be added to the general fund of the University; and the remainder of the £50,000 is to be employed in founding sixteen 'Vans Dunlop Scholarships', of the annual value of £100 each, tenable for three years. It is also provided by the will that the first six scholarships created shall be for students of medicine, while the others are to be equally divided amongst students of the classes of chemistry, English literature, classics, political economy, logic and moral philosophy, natural philosophy, mathematics, natural history, and engineering. These scholarships in medicine will be the most splendid encouragements that that hitherto poorly endowed faculty can offer to earnest students of medicine.

There have been many eminent recipients of Vans Dunlop Scholarships over the years, including pathologist James Lorrain Smith (1862–1931, also a Ferguson recipient), pathologist Sir Robert Muir

(1864–1959), philosopher and politician Charles Mackinnon Douglas (1865–1924), pathologist Sir Sydney Alfred Smith (1883–1969), pathologist and surgeon Dr J. Argyll Campbell (1884–1944, twice Vans Dunlop Scholar) and Lord Advocate Lord Gordon Stott (1909–99), and it is difficult to select just one to profile here.

Professor James Duguid (1919–2012) received a Vans Dunlop Scholarship in 1944. He was awarded his MB ChB in 1942 before graduating with a BSc with first class honours in 1943. He joined the University's bacteriology department in 1944 where he produced research that revolutionised the understanding of penicillin. His groundbreaking findings were not immediately recognised when they were published in the *Edinburgh Medical Journal* in 1946, only receiving attention eleven years later, after being briefly acknowledged by an American research team who gained international renown when they produced similar results.

Duguid graduated as a Doctor of Medicine in 1949, with a gold medal-winning thesis on the transmission of respiratory tract pathogenic bacteria. His publications continued to significantly advance understanding of the field of bacteriology, including the revelation in 1955 of certain transmission mechanisms of all too familiar infections *E.coli* and *Salmonella*.

Following Duguid's death in 2012, Professor John Gerald Collee CBE spoke of his colleague's remarkable achievements, noting in his obituary that

> [h]is work on penicillin is not widely known and he did not get the credit for some of his original (and correct) theories on the mode of action of the first, and still the best, of our antibiotics. He generated many new approaches to the airborne spread of infection and he was responsible for some of our important knowledge of antisepsis and disinfection.

### *The Stewart Bequest and Sir James Young Simpson*

One name-specific bursary was the Stewart Bequest, founded in 1810 by the Rev. James Stewart, from South Carolina. He specified that preference was to be given to applicants with the surname Stewart, but bursaries were also open to those named Simpson, the maiden name of his mother. This proved fortunate for one applicant – and for humanity – as the recipient went on to make an enormous contribution to medicine worldwide.

Born in Bathgate, West Lothian in 1811, James Simpson entered the University at the age of fourteen. He successfully applied for a Stewart Bursary as he began his second year. Although Simpson completed his exams at the age of eighteen, he was too young to graduate, and had to wait two years before being granted his licence to practise medicine. Following his graduation in 1832, Simpson's professional progress was rapid. He began lecturing at the University, was elected senior President of the Royal Medical Society of Edinburgh in 1835, was appointed to the Chair of Medicine and Midwifery at the age of twenty-eight and pioneered the use of anaesthetics in surgery and midwifery. Simpson became Queen Victoria's physician in 1847, and discovered the anaesthetic properties of chloroform that same year.

Sir James Young Simpson, painted by Sir John Watson Gordon. Watson Gordon was himself a major benefactor to the University

It is this discovery of chloroform and its subsequent promotion in the medical profession for which Simpson is best known, though he introduced many other innovations that advanced the field of medicine, particularly midwifery. Famously, his discovery of chloroform came about during one of his evening sessions testing out new chemicals with two colleagues. Together they inhaled chloroform and apparently felt quite wonderful, before the anaesthetic effects knocked them unconscious, fortunately only for the night.

This chloroform bottle, in its leather case, was owned by James Young Simpson

Simpson faced opposition from the Church and the general medical profession for his discovery, who thought it dangerous, unnatural and even against the teachings of the Bible. The use of chloroform by Queen Victoria during the birth of her eighth child, Prince Leopold, is generally thought to have led to public, professional and theological acceptance of the chemical's anaesthetic function.

Andrew Grant

Simpson was elected President of the Royal College of Physicians in 1849 and President of the Royal Society of Edinburgh in 1852. He received his knighthood in 1866 and was granted the freedom of the city of Edinburgh in 1869.

### Andrew Grant and Edinburgh College of Art

Students at Edinburgh College of Art (ECA), which merged with the University in 2011, still benefit from the generosity of Andrew Grant (1830–1924), a merchant and Liberal MP. In addition to giving £10,000 towards the building of the main ECA building which was constructed between 1907 and 1909, Grant left a substantial bequest to fund travelling scholarships for art students. Beneficiaries have included Anne Redpath and John Bellany, and a project to create 'Schools Beautiful' in the 1930s saw students funded to produce work in primary schools across the city.

Part of the 'Schools Beautiful' project, John Maxwell's mural *Children's Games* incorporated ideas suggested by children at Craigmillar School. Tom Whalen's fountain *Mother and Child* was unveiled at Prestonfield School in June 1935

A. Theo Marshall produced this report in 1939 following his completion of an Andrew Grant Bequest travelling scholarship

### GENEROSITY REPAID

The majority of awards to students are made with 'no strings attached' other than continued academic progress, but it is particularly pleasing when the recipient of a much-needed award decides to recognise that gift later in life by 'repaying' it, as demonstrated by the following vignettes.

#### Bidder and the Jardine Bursary

One such was George Parker Bidder, who in turn set up the Jardine Bursary. His letter to the University was reported in the minutes of 24 December 1846:

> George Parker Bidder, Esq. Civil Engineer residing near London who, feeling 'deeply indebted to that seminary for the great benefit derived by me from my attendance at various classes therein' wished to establish a bursary in memory of Sir Henry Jardin, who long filled the office of King's Remembrancer for Scotland. This was 'to be enjoyed by any one Student for a period of not exceeding four years … the only qualifications requisite for holding said Scholarship or Bursary to be, that the recipient is a native of Scotland, of good character, of promising talent, and of known diligence, and that he really requires aid to enable him with ease to attain a proper university education. And in founding said Scholarship or Bursary, [I] have entertained the hope, that some of the recipients, who may be successful in their pursuits in after life (as I have been), through grateful recollection of the measure, in which this has been promoted by the advantages thus enjoyed by those of a University Education may, in like manner as I am about to do, express their gratitude to their *Alma Mater*, and so aid the progress and advancement of others who may follow in circumstances with themselves'.

George Parker Bidder

Bidder's history is an interesting one. At an early age, he was known for his exceptional ability for calculation. 'His skill was first noticed when, after he was in bed, he heard his elders trying to work out what they would get from the butcher for their pig, and impatiently shouted the correct answer down the stairs.' Frequently rewarded for demonstrating his skills whilst sitting at the local blacksmith's, he soon became known as the 'Calculating Boy' or 'Calculating Prodigy', and was exhibited as such (for a fee) by his stonemason father, William Bidder, at various fairs and shows around the country. In Edinburgh in 1819, he was noticed by Sir Henry Jardine, a lawyer and King's Remembrancer for Scotland. Jardine paid for George's private tuition for a year, and then for his study of mathematical and natural philosophy at the University. There Bidder befriended Robert Stephenson (designer of 'the Rocket' and son of 'Father of Railways' George Stephenson), with whom he later worked on the Stockton and Darlington Railway. After his graduation from the University he worked at the Ordnance Survey (a position found by Jardine) until 1824. In addition to working on railways, canals and trams, Bidder was instrumental in the development of the telegraph and the eventual development of transatlantic cables. He is said to have been responsible for recommending the employment of female telegraph operators, the first 'office' jobs for women.

Bidder's appreciation of the support he received from Jardine, and his subsequent establishment of a bursary honouring him, is a fine example of generosity being recognised and repaid.

### Chrissie Miller

A similar story of generosity repaid is that of Christina (Chrissie) Miller. She received the University's Vans Dunlop Scholarship and undertook a four-year diploma at Edinburgh in 1917 combined with a three-year degree at Heriot-Watt. At this time, university courses usually lasting three terms were compressed into two because of the war, yet she managed to be a first-class student at both institutions. Her subsequent PhD in chemistry at Edinburgh – at a time when relatively few women were attending university, and very few of those were becoming involved in scientific research – was aided by a Carnegie Research Scholarship. During the Second World War, Miller 'prepared and equipped a laboratory for rapid detection of war gases, devised a scheme for twenty-four of these, prepared all the reagents, and tested the scheme extensively'. In 1949, she became one of the first five women, and the only chemist of those, to be elected to the Royal Society of Edinburgh. After her death in July 2001, just a few weeks short of her 102nd birthday, the University received from Miller a bequest of £246,000 to be put towards a bursary scheme at the School of Chemistry. Over the following five years this funded several students in their postgraduate studies.

Chrissie Miller in her laboratory at Heriot-Watt College

INTO THE TWENTIETH CENTURY

Appointed in 1876 to make recommendations for Scottish universities, the Royal Commission produced a report in 1878 that finally became law as the second Universities (Scotland) Act 1889. The primary achievement of this Act was arguably granting universities the power 'to admit women to graduation in such Faculty or Faculties as the said Court may think fit', although it was not until 1892 that the University of Edinburgh enabled the graduation of women. But the Act also made reference to bursaries, as according to the Royal Commission's reports of 1831, 1858 and 1889, these were 'universally inadequate in value'. As a result of the Act, the University Commissioners published the *List of Deeds of Foundation of Bursaries, Scholarships, Fellowships, &c. in the University of Edinburgh* (1891). This featured 111 entries, a testament to the effectiveness of the Act in expanding funding for students.

The twentieth century saw further investment in student funding nationally, with 60,000 Scottish students being assisted with payment of fees over the forty years to 1941. The Educational Endowments (Scotland) Act set up a new Commission in 1928 to look at schemes for rationalising and administering educational trusts, and the University Court and Senatus took full advantage of this, creating 'an elaborate and far-reaching scheme ... for the revision and reorganisation of its bursaries and scholarships'. The Edinburgh University Fellowships, Scholarships and Bursaries Scheme, 1931 came into force in July 1932 and resulted in

> a larger and more evenly distributed number of Bursaries for award to entrants who show promise, while at the same time [safeguarding] the interest of the localities favoured by the original founders ... Above all, the desire of the founders to benefit individual students has been respected; none of the funds has been diverted to any other purpose.

### DEVELOPMENTS IN THE TWENTY-FIRST CENTURY

As major employers increasingly recognise the importance of contributing to international development, there is a welcome increase in sponsorship by business and industry. At the same time, recognition of the need to make a university education possible for students regardless of social background or geographic origin has led to new types of bursary.

#### *Corporate sponsorship*

Since 2003, the Coca-Cola Foundation has given $2.25m annually, through the Coca-Cola International Scholarships: Scholarships Change Lives Program. The Scholarship provides full tuition fees and living costs for the best international students to come to Edinburgh. Michal Kochman is one such student, coming from Gdansk, Poland in 2006 to study towards an MSc in Chemistry. He recalls the difficulties he faced when having to become financially independent:

> my mother suffers from nearly complete paralysis as a result of spinal cord injury, and needs professional care at all times. In Poland, this is not provided by the state, and a nurse is hired to tend to her. This leaves my father as the only person in work in the family. In consequence, taking

up the Chemistry course at the University of Edinburgh … would have been out of the question if not for the Coca-Cola Scholarship.

Michal subsequently went on to study for a PhD in Chemistry at the University. The distinction of University Benefactor was bestowed on the Coca-Cola Foundation in 2009.

### *Access Bursaries*

That survey in the 1860s which showed that the majority of students (all men, of course, at that time) were 'predominantly middle class' also noted that the availability of charitable funds enabled others to benefit from education at the University of Edinburgh. Widening access to education is as important now as it was then, and one of the many successes of the recent 'Edinburgh Campaign' has been the extension of the Access Bursaries Scheme. In 2013, over 700 students were receiving support for the duration of their degrees, with more than 200 new Access Bursaries awarded to incoming students that year.

One donor who helped make this happen is Mr Christopher Stone, who expressed the view that 'It would be unhealthy if prestigious universities found themselves with only students from privileged backgrounds'. Mr Stone's family was from Nazi Germany and unable to support his psychology studies at the University of Edinburgh, but the state paid his fees and provided a maintenance grant. He now helps those from disadvantaged backgrounds attain their university goals by personally funding thirteen bursaries.

'Giving for this purpose is hugely rewarding,' says Mr Stone. 'These are people from difficult backgrounds with many impediments to getting to university. If I am able to help them, that makes me very happy. It is all the reward one needs.'

### *Specific scholarships*

Sometimes, funds are collected to recognise a particular event or anniversary. The Africa LLM/MSc Tercentenary Scholarship was made possible by many generous donations from friends and former pupils of the Law School. Its creation formed part of the tercentenary celebrations in 2007, marking the 300th anniversary of the School's first Chair in Law, the Regius Chair of Public Law and the Law of Nature and Nations.

Widening participation lies at the heart of the School and the University's agenda; a core aim being to ensure that no student is deterred from entering the University by financial barriers. The School has strong and historic links with Africa with regard to both teaching and research. A key objective of the Tercentenary Scholarship is to celebrate these links and to underscore the commitment of the scholarly community to the principles of equality, inclusion and diversity.

The first recipient of the Scholarship was Baboki Dambe from Botswana, who joined the Law School in September 2009 to study international law. He graduated with the degree of LLM with Distinction at the awards ceremony in November 2010.

### LOOKING TO THE FUTURE

With the exception of a brief period in the twentieth century when, for UK students at least, fees were not charged and a mean-tested grant for living costs was available, gaining a university education has always represented a financial sacrifice for all but the very wealthy. But it is clear that, in Scotland at least, there has always been an awareness that education should not just exist for the financially privileged. The importance of bursaries, prizes and scholarships was recognised early, and the need for them grows annually as the University seeks to educate an ever wider pool of global citizens.

In 2003, the University established a dedicated Scholarships and Student Funding Office, one of the first within a UK institution, to provide an overview of all the funding available across the University. The office provides expert advice to applicants and administers all of the main bursary and scholarship schemes offered by the University.

In recent years the University has greatly expanded the number of scholarships and bursaries that it offers. This has included prestigious international awards such as the Chevening Scholarships, and scholarships funded by the Scottish, UK and foreign governments. University-funded awards also assist masters students from emerging international markets, such as India, China and Latin America, while the innovative Principal's Career Development Scholarship offers

PhD scholars exciting career development opportunities in addition to a generous financial package. The last fundraising campaign significantly over-achieved on the target for bursaries and scholarships thanks to the support of many donors.

The University has also used bursaries, prizes and scholarships to respond positively to legislative changes within Scottish higher education. The introduction by the Scottish Government in 2012 of the higher rate of fee for students who normally live in England, Wales and Northern Ireland prompted the introduction of the most generous bursary package by a UK institution. The 'University of Edinburgh Bursary' ensured that this legislative change did not act as a significant barrier to students, thus maintaining a diverse and talented student population.

One of the impressive successes of the University's recently completed fundraising campaign was the huge support of donors to the Access Bursaries mentioned above. Donors range from individuals to corporations. Some of the most recent corporate bursaries have new twists; recognising how hard it can be for some students to gain experience and develop networks, some donors now provide mentoring and work experience as well as financial support. Some even require recipients to engage in volunteering, which develops external skills and a sense of 'giving back' whilst still at the University. The Lloyds Banking Scholarships are an excellent example of this new approach.

Scholarships were also a major success story from the fundraising campaign. Masters programmes are increasingly important to students, allowing them to follow a focused career-oriented programme and thus setting them up for employment. There are now over 7,000 masters students annually. Many individuals and companies have supported students on masters programmes, some of them focusing on areas of current global concern. Deutsche Post DHL Scholarships are one example of this, supporting programmes in the Edinburgh Centre for Carbon Innovation (ECCI), the broader work of which is covered in Chapter 4. Students are also supported across the University in their PhD studies by a variety of sponsors, and some examples of this are also covered in Chapter 4.

As the global marketplace for higher education becomes more competitive, the University will continue to develop its use of bursaries and scholarships to ensure that it can attract the very brightest and best students regardless of their personal circumstances. In that respect it is following the traditions set by John Knox, Donald Grant and others many years ago.

Some of the University's scholars who attended a dinner to welcome them to Edinburgh

# 6

## Museums and Collections

THE UNIVERSITY IS VERY FORTUNATE in having several collections which are already recognised as being of world importance, as well as some which are much less well-known. Far from being dusty accumulations of forgotten objects, the University collections are used by students and staff for academic purposes, as well as by visiting researchers. Many of the collections are also open to the public, either on a regular basis or for specific events, and help to inform the public about the work going on in the University. The stories behind several of the collections – how they came together in the first place and how they subsequently arrived at the University of Edinburgh – are worthy of a book in their own right. The collections range in size and importance, with some being grouped together within University museums, and each holds a significance in the University's history and an implication for its future. Within the Estates and Buildings offices, display cases containing ephemera such as a very early 15-amp plug, a section of water pipe made in the seventeenth century from an elm trunk, a broken cast-iron banister or the invoices for building materials for Old College all speak to the history of Edinburgh as a city and the development of technological improvements which were affecting the population as a whole. Other collections are truly international, bringing together some of the finest examples of objects of a particular type drawn from across the world. This chapter looks at examples from a few of the University's collections.

This apparently amateur cardboard model of Old College was made in 1825 and shows the clock tower which was never built; it is one of several historical artefacts held by Estates and Buildings

## LIBRARY COLLECTIONS

### The Clement Litill Collection

The University Library is arguably older than the University itself. Clement Litill (or Litil or Little – spellings vary) bequeathed 276 volumes in 1580, three years before the Tounis College came into existence. His books were thus the first in the library of the new establishment. Covering both Catholic and Protestant theology and humanist scholarship, the collection contains several outstanding individual items. Each book is stamped 'I am gevin to Edinburgh & Kirk of God be Maister Clement Litil Thair to Reman. 1580'.

A bookstamp from a volume in Clement Litill's bequest

*The William Drummond Collection*

William Drummond of Hawthornden (1585–1649) was one of the University's early students, graduating in 1605 before proceeding to further study in Bourges and in Paris. A book collector as well as a poet and man of letters, Drummond donated over 600 books during his lifetime. His gifts to the University included two Shakespeare quartos, a complete copy of John Derrick's *Image of Irelande* and pamphlets encouraging the colonisation of Nova Scotia.

A Shakespeare quarto from the William Drummond Collection

David Laing in his study

Darwin's signed photograph, part of the Heiskell Darwin Collection

### The David Laing Collection

David Laing (1793–1878) was the son of an Edinburgh bookseller. He became the leading Scottish expert on early books and manuscripts, travelling across Europe in the quest for additions to his collection. After his death, his library of printed books was sold, but his collections of art works and objects are now held in the National Galleries of Scotland and the National Museums of Scotland. His manuscript collection was gifted to the University, and the Laing Collection includes many items of international importance. Early Islamic manuscripts, over 3,000 charters, letters by kings and queens of Scotland and England, and Laing's personal papers including correspondence with William and Dorothy Wordsworth all form part of the collection.

### The Heiskell Darwin Collection

A more recent and very welcome addition to the Main Library's holding is the Heiskell Darwin Collection, which came to the University in

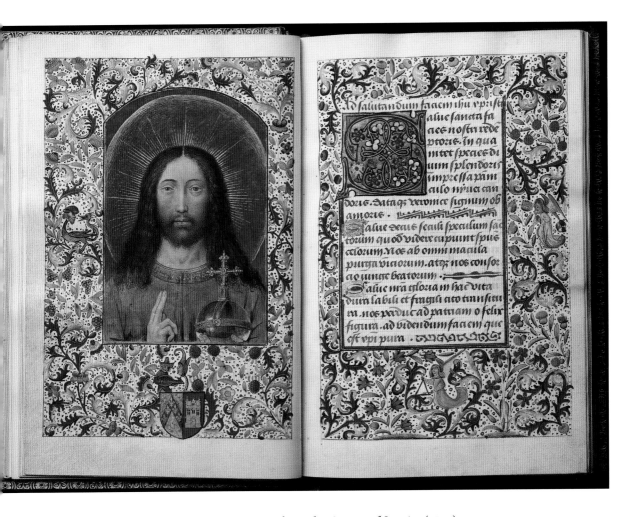

2012. Fine copies of the first edition of *On the Origin of Species* (1859) joined other important early editions to form a collection of over 100 volumes of lifetime editions of Darwin's works.

Part of the James Cathcart White bequest, this Book of Hours was written in the southern Netherlands in the fifteenth century

### The James Cathcart White Bequest

James Cathcart White (1853–1943) was an Edinburgh graduate and advocate, and left the Main Library not just a fine collection of books, but a significant sum of money which is still used to purchase books and manuscripts today. The collection includes a copy of Cicero's *Epistolae ad Familiares*, printed on vellum in 1469 in Venice.

MUSICAL COLLECTIONS

### John Donaldson Collection

John Donaldson was appointed professor of music at the University of Edinburgh in 1845. He was very forward thinking in his approach to teaching and to the needs of music within the University as a whole. His work and tenure included the building of the Reid Concert Hall as a teaching building for music, for housing the music library and as a space for his museum of instruments. This original museum space is still used for that purpose. Money both for the building of the hall and for acquiring objects for the collection came from the bequest of General John Reid (1721–1807), a military man who was a keen musician and amateur composer, though the professor of music had to take the University to court to force them to use the bequest to provide a building as Reid had intended. A series of photographs which survive from the nineteenth century show the collection *in situ* as Donaldson intended it, and from these the important role that the collection played in the day-to-day teaching and education of music students during this period is very apparent.

General John Reid, painted by George Watson, and the Reid Concert Hall

In many ways Donaldson appears to have been attracted to the more unusual: examples include a violin without sides, now believed to have been made by a member of the Bassano family in London during the second half of the sixteenth century, an English guitar with a key mechanism and several *pochettes* – small violins for dancing-masters which, as the name suggests, fitted into the master's pocket when not in use.

### The Raymond Russell Collection

In the early 1960s, Raymond Russell, a keen antiquarian who had amassed an excellent collection of early keyboard instruments (in addition to writing *The Harpsichord and Clavichord*, still the standard starting textbook even today), was looking for a permanent home for his collection. He approached the University of Edinburgh who immediately expressed positive interest, including the purchase of St Cecilia's Hall as a building to house the collection. Unfortunately Russell died in 1964, prior to the finalisation of the gift, but his mother pursued discussions with the University, eventually giving nineteen instruments, the substantial part of his collection, to the University. Subsequently the University purchased two further instruments which Mrs Russell had retained following the gift, bringing the number to twenty-one. Russell had started his collection in the 1940s, at a time when there was little competition for such instruments or appreciation of their historical value. Many of his instruments are amongst the finest surviving examples, including the only extant Ruckers double-manual harpsichord with unaltered keyboards, and the 1769 Taskin harpsichord – the model for the first revival instrument in 1882 and surely the most copied and famous harpsichord in the world. Russell was particularly interested in northern continental instruments, and the Ruckers family (including a nephew, Ioannes Couchet) is the early-keyboard equivalent of the Stradivaris. Russell had four instruments by the family, plus another which he thought was a Couchet but was subsequently shown to be an eighteenth-century French instrument which had been altered (by Pascal Taskin, the maker of the 1769 instrument) by changing some initials from IG (for Jean Goermans) to IC, presumably in order to increase its value.

The University continued collecting keyboard instruments following the Raymond Russell gift, including obtaining several instruments

St Cecilia's Hall houses an
internationally important collection
of keyboard instruments

by donation. By the early 2000s, the number of instruments had increased to around sixty.

### The Rodger Mirrey Collection

The second major gift of keyboard instruments was the Rodger Mirrey Collection, given to the University in 2005. Dr Rodger Mirrey started collecting in the mid-1960s, at a time when instruments, especially good ones, were harder to obtain than in Russell's day. Despite this, Mirrey amassed a substantial collection, with particular emphasis on Italian instruments, early English harpsichords and clavichords. His collection includes the oldest dated instrument in the University's music collections, a Venetian harpsichord of 1574 (and thus older than the University itself). The early English instruments include examples by Barton, Slade, Crang and Wilbrook, and together they form a substantial portion of surviving pre-1750 English harpsichords. The collection itself comprised twenty-two instruments, actually larger than the Russell gift, and there was essentially no overlap between the two major gifts. Together they have given the University a keyboard collection with what is almost certainly the widest scope in the world. The instruments continue to be used by researchers, some of them are played by musicians and all are enjoyed by the many visitors to the collection.

### Anne Macaulay Collection of Musical Instruments

Anne Macaulay had a special interest in fretted stringed instruments, in particular instruments of the guitar and lute family. A member of the Fife-based Russell family of paper-makers and a professional pilot, she started collecting in the 1960s, a time when interest in these instruments was particularly limited, therefore enabling her to amass a collection of fine examples. She was an active amateur player and was particularly interested in examples which were in, or could be re-stored to, playing condition. Her collection was gifted to the University in two groups. It includes a number of early baroque guitars from Italy (including an example attributed to Matteo Sellas of Venice, another by Pfanzelt which was converted in the historical period to a metal-strung *battente* and an example by Pietro Railich with the back, sides and neck decorated in very fine parquetry work). Also included are instruments from Germany and France, a six-course Spanish guitar by Pagés of Cádiz – one of the finest decorated of its type – and a range of early-nineteenth-century guitars by other leading makers such as Fabricatore, Panormo, Lacôte, Soirot and Guiot. Later instruments by Martin and Manuel Ramirez are included, the latter being built at the time the workshop was near its pinnacle, having one of its instruments used by Andrés Segovia.

A small selection from the Sir Nicholas Shackleton Collection

### Sir Nicholas Shackleton Collection

Professor Sir Nicholas Shackleton (1937–2006) was a highly distinguished scientist at Cambridge whose work was both groundbreaking and award-winning. His musical instrument collection – principally one of clarinets – was approached in the same manner. It is one of the outstanding woodwind collections, in terms of both size and scope, to be privately amassed and was collected over a period of forty years. The collection came to the University as part of a bequest following Shackleton's death.

The clarinets range in date from around 1740 – not long after the invention of the instrument – to comparatively modern times. The clarinet is represented in all of its forms, including outstanding examples by makers through its history from all of the leading countries of manufacture. Instruments which were in some way unusual – perhaps in their choice of material or key mechanism – form part of the collection, which therefore includes clarinets made from brass, a black-coloured plastic called ebonite and clear plastic.

Wind and brass instruments
on display

The entire collection consists of some 880 instruments in total. Over 800 are clarinets and basset horns, along with around forty flutes and examples of other instruments including oboes, bassoons and French horns, among others. The clarinets cover all sizes from the largest contrabass instruments to the smallest examples in high A (essentially an octave above the 'normal' clarinet). All major traditions are represented, usually by the finest examples of those locations and time periods.

### Frank Tomes Collection

The Frank Tomes Collection is small when compared to other wind and brass collections, but shows a high level of connoisseurship in its compilation. Although it does not represent everything that Tomes himself collected – the final gift (following his death) being a selection which would best represent the intentions of Tomes as a collector – the quality of the objects shows the eye of someone who, in addition to being able to acquire the finest instruments, was also a highly skilled professional brass instrument maker. This was something he started as a second career in the mid-1980s, initially making sackbuts (early trombones) in the Christopher Monk workshop, and later also making natural and slide trumpets under his own name.

The collection is not restricted to or focused on a single type of instrument, although brass instruments are predominant. Even there they span the range of examples, including the bugle, serpent, ophicleide, cornopean, cornet, vocal horn, saxhorn, clavicor, tuba, trumpet and trombone. Non-brass examples include non-western wind instruments, the clarinet and a Turkish crescent – a large percussion instrument with numerous bells which went by the popular name of the 'jingling johnny'.

### James Blades Collection

Perhaps no musician has to cover as wide-ranging a collection of instruments as a percussionist. Orchestral writing makes use of both tuned (xylophone, glockenspiel, tubular bells, tuned timpani) and untuned (cymbals, kettledrums, sidedrums, bass drum, triangle) instruments and will frequently call for a wide palette of sounds according to the piece of music. A typical orchestra will often require more than one percussionist to provide all that is asked by the composer. Even percussionists who play other types of music are required to play numerous objects – a drum kit may be augmented by temple blocks, cowbells, cymbals, bells and gongs, and frequently requires both hands and feet to play simultaneously.

The Blades Collection brings together the multitude of instruments that were owned by James Blades, the leading London-based orchestral and studio percussionist of the mid-twentieth century. Perhaps the most important job Blades held was comparatively simple – every few months he would go into a studio with his tam-tam (one of several he owned) and strike it. The resulting recordings have been heard at the start of numerous films produced by the Rank Organisation.

### Bagpipe Collection

From 2008 to 2013, the musical instrument collection had a Heritage Lottery Fund 'Collecting Cultures' project in which the fund paid a grant towards the purchase and display of bagpipes. The bagpipe is traditionally thought of as a Scottish instrument, immediately conjuring up images of tartan-clad pipers marching (often in bands) at the Edinburgh Tattoo and other ceremonial events. Although this image is, of course, legitimate, it represents only one aspect of the British pipe tradition.

Whereas the highland 'great pipes' are particularly associated with Scotland and its musical heritage, and are often the only pipes the layperson may immediately think of, there are numerous other types which have co-existed with the highland pipes, usually for use in greatly different contexts. Scotland itself has several types such as the lowland pipes and border pipes – smaller chamber instruments which still have a small but thriving following. Outside Scotland the Northumbrian pipes have a solid tradition, and Britain can also lay claim to pastoral pipes and possibly to the 'union' or uillean pipes which are particularly well known in Ireland.

In all, the Collecting Cultures project resulted in some eighteen sets of pipes and nine practice chanters coming into the collection.

## POLISH SCHOOL OF MEDICINE (1941–9)

The Nazi invasion of Poland in 1939 effectively destroyed academic life there and many Poles, including senior academics, arrived in Britain with the Polish army. In an act of great compassion and generosity the University of Edinburgh facilitated the setting-up of the Polish School of Medicine within its walls. Originally intended to meet the needs of students and doctors in the Polish armed forces, the School accepted civilians from the outset, and by the time it closed in 1949, over 330 students had matriculated, 227 had graduated MB ChB and nineteen had obtained a doctorate or MD. Only a few of the Polish School's graduates returned to Poland after the war. Over half remained in the UK, though some emigrated to Europe, the USA, Canada, Australia or elsewhere. Students studying in the Polish School followed a Polish curriculum, were taught mainly in Polish and were awarded Polish degrees. The graduates and staff of the Polish School maintained strong links with the University, holding five-yearly reunions in Edinburgh from 1966 onwards. In 1986, they established the Polish School of Medicine Memorial Fund. In the same year, the Polish School of Medicine Historical Collection was established by the late Dr Wiktor Tomaszewski, a former member of staff at the Polish School and general medical practitioner in Edinburgh. Many of the artefacts in the collection were gifted by Dr Tomaszewski himself and by Polish medical academies, grateful former students, staff and graduates of the Polish School and their families and friends.

Since 2004, the Chancellor's Building, the University's Medical Academic Centre at Little France, has been home to the collection, which is eclectic in nature. It encompasses over 100 medals, many of them Polish and of medical interest, and also the military medals and awards belonging to the late Professor Antoni Jurasz, the first Dean of the School, and to one of its graduates, Dr Stanley Kryszek. In addition it contains wartime memorabilia, books about the Polish School of Medicine, photographs,

Plaque commemorating the inauguration of the Polish School of Medicine

paintings, and pen and ink drawings by Polish artist Josef Młynarski of key University and Edinburgh buildings with medical links. The collection also includes sculptures by Professor Jakub Rostowski, the third and last Dean of the School. Taken as a whole, the collection tells the story of the Polish School from its beginnings up until the present day.

ART COLLECTION

*University Art Collection*

The University holds around 2,500 works of art, comprising the University of Edinburgh's original fine art collection (which spans some 400 years of collecting) and the collection of prints, drawings, paintings and sculpture held by Edinburgh College of Art. This latter collection joined the University Art Collection in 2011 when the institutions merged. Some works in the collection have been commissioned, some purchased, others were acquired to decorate University rooms and, crucially, certain collections came to the University as bequests. As a result, the collection has its own unique character.

Particularly with the addition of the Edinburgh College of Art collection, the University Art Collection is notable for an emphasis on Scottish art. This includes an extensive range of historical and contemporary Scottish portraits featuring major historical figures and past Principals and professors of the University. Modern Scottish art is also well represented with a significant collection of works by William Johnstone and featuring pieces by many others including Joan Eardley, F. C. B. Cadell and William MacTaggart.

A large proportion of the University Art Collection is on display throughout the campus, enhancing the public, staff and student spaces. A number of works from the Torrie Collection of Dutch and Flemish masters are also on long-term loan to the National Galleries of Scotland where they are enjoyed by audiences of nearly a million people per year. The principal areas of display on campus include the Talbot Rice Gallery, Edinburgh College of Art, Old College, Playfair Library, Raeburn Room, the Main Library, New College, McEwan Hall and the Royal (Dick) School of Veterinary Studies.

The collection is vital as a teaching resource and is actively used in seminars and lecture programmes, for both art history and fine

Joan Eardley – *January Flow Tide*

art students. New interpretations and collaborations are sought so that collections are displayed in fresh and exciting ways, introducing contemporary insights to invigorate debate, with the University community central to those conversations.

The University has been fortunate enough to have received many bequests of significant art works throughout its history. The size and circumstances of these gifts vary greatly and the stories behind them add further richness to the overall history of the Art Collection. Consequently, the collection itself is subdivided to retain the provenance collections and acknowledge the donors who were generous enough to gift them.

### Torrie Collection

The Torrie Collection is the University's signature collection of art works. Donated to the University by Sir James Erskine, 3rd Baronet of Torrie, it comprises some seventy-nine pieces. It consists mainly of seventeenth-century Dutch paintings, but with Flemish and Italian Renaissance works also peppering the collection. The group has a particular selection within it of outstanding significance, with the sixteenth-century *Anatomical Figure of a Horse* by Giambologna and Jacob Isaacksz van Ruisdael's *The Banks of a River* two of the undoubted highlights. As well as being shown extensively within the University itself, works from the Torrie Collection have been loaned to exhibitions in London, Vienna, Los Angeles and Madrid, promoting on a global stage the Art Collection and the University itself.

James Erskine was born in Torrie House, Fife, in 1772 and, as well as being an accomplished art collector, was a highly successful career soldier. Rising to the rank of lieutenant general, he served with Wellington and it was through Erskine's military service that some of the works that now form the Torrie Collection would have been acquired. Indeed, it was common for high-ranking military men to collect antiques and works of art to populate their residences, and Dutch art was the emerging fashion of the time. After the French Revolution and Napoleon's subsequent invasion of Holland, Dutch art entered the London art market for the first time. As well as the Duke of Wellington himself, many of the people in Erskine's social and professional circles were keen art collectors; between 1802 and 1804 Erskine was aide-de-camp to King George III and also a friend of the Prince Regent, who himself was a major collector of Dutch landscapes.

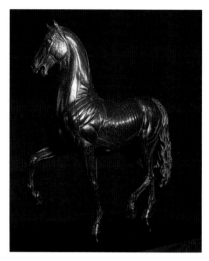

Giambologna's anatomical figure
of a horse

Jacob Isaacksz van Ruisdael –
*The Banks of a River*, 1649

The collection was built in the early decades of the 1800s and displayed primarily in Erskine's London residence. In his will in 1824, he stipulated that the works in his London home would be bequeathed to the University of Edinburgh upon his death, which occurred the following year. The collection eventually came into the University in 1836 and, a few years later, was loaned to the Royal Institution; it then passed from there to its successor body, the National Galleries of Scotland. The majority of the collection was given back to the University in 1954, with a further small group of works returning in 1983.

Why Erskine chose the University of Edinburgh for his collection is not entirely clear, but there are key events and characters that offer

tantalising clues to his motivations. Many of the great museum institutions that we know today were founded on the personal collections of the great philanthropists of the 1800s. In 1826, Sir George Beaumont donated his collection of Italian, Dutch, Flemish and British art to the nation – a collection that would go on to form the National Gallery in London. Similarly, in Scotland, the Hunterian was founded in 1807 following the bequest of a collection of scientific instruments, historical artefacts and art works by Dr William Hunter in 1783. Erskine no doubt had the precedent of the Hunterian in mind when deciding on the location of his collection and it is possible that he wished Edinburgh to receive a similar gift of art works.

The art historian Duncan MacMillan has argued that William Playfair was also central to the negotiations with Erskine on the final location of his art collection. At the time, Playfair was involved in the commission of what is now known as Old College and initial plans may have included a space for the display of the collection. Indeed, Erskine stated in his will that it was his wish that the collection would 'lay the foundation of a Gallery for the encouragement of the Fine Arts'. Initially, the gallery space within Old College did not transpire; however, parts of the collection were eventually transferred to the Talbot Rice Gallery, where displays of key Torrie works adorn the balcony of the Georgian Gallery. If conversations between Erskine and Playfair did in fact take place, then it is fitting that the collection often resides there over 150 years after its donation.

The story of the Torrie Collection does not end, however, with merely its display and appreciation. The collection actively drives teaching within the University – postgraduate study and academic research still centre on this collection, continually re-evaluating and refreshing our understanding whilst providing an important teaching resource. Indeed, there is still much to discover in the Torrie Collection, particularly in the history of Erskine's collecting and the provenance of some key works.

*The Hope Scott Collection*

Much like the relationship between William Playfair and James Erskine, the connection between key individuals can lead to the birth of a collection as well as the decision to gift it. The Hope Scott Collection is a fantastic example of a friendship driving a collection of art on the one side, and the creation of art on the other.

William Johnstone's portrait of
Hope Scott

Samuel Peploe – *Cyclamen*

Hope Scott was the only daughter of Henry Johnston Younger of Harmeny, near Balerno, of the long-established brewing dynasty. In 1918, she married Charles William Montagu Douglas Scott, a grandson of the 5th Duke of Buccleuch. Scott met the Scottish abstract painter William Johnstone at one of his exhibitions in Newcastle in 1969. She already had a keen eye for art and had been acquiring pieces for some time, but her introduction to Johnstone began a love of his work that would last for the rest of her life. Johnstone and Scott became close friends and, almost immediately after their meeting, she began to collect his work. In all, the Hope Scott Collection contains fifty-nine pieces by Johnstone – one of the largest representations of his work in a public collection. This was not merely a one-sided relationship, however. Johnstone stated in his autobiography that Scott was a major influence behind his rekindled desire to work; she was therefore an active influence on Johnstone's creative output.

As well as a healthy spine of works by William Johnstone, the collection contains pieces by some of the twentieth century's most illustrious names. *Going to the Fair* by Pablo Picasso is a key work in the University Art Collection, as are paintings by Samuel Peploe, Pierre Bonnard and Max Ernst and works on paper by Alan Davie, F. C. B. Cadell and Sir William Gillies. The collection shows Scott's varied tastes and also, particularly in the inclusion of Picasso, Ernst and Johnstone himself, a keen eye for Modernism and abstraction.

The decision to donate the collection to the University of Edinburgh is much like the story of the collection itself – centred on the friendship between Scott and Johnstone. The principal reason for Scott bequeathing the collection

Pablo Picasso – *Going to the Fair*

was the University's decision to honour Johnstone with an honorary degree in 1980. Moved by the recognition of Johnstone's achievements as an artist – rather than the educator he was predominantly known as in England – Scott informed the University of her intention to gift part of her personal collection of art works. In 1983, Scott gifted four paintings by Johnstone to mark the University's quatercentenary – one for each of the University's centuries in existence. After Scott's death in 1989, the remainder of the collection was transferred.

As well as signifying a long-standing friendship, the Hope Scott Collection is testament to Scott's philanthropic spirit, which continues to this day. As well as donating a significant collection of art works to the University, the Hope Scott Trust supports young artists and musicians in their early careers, providing support for exhibitions and training.

### Individual artists: Talbot Rice Memorial Collection

The Talbot Rice Memorial Collection is a touching example of a collection forming to commemorate the life and achievements of one man and highlights the unique character that the University Art Collection enjoys. Consisting of some twenty oil and watercolour paintings, this collection was created to honour the late professor of fine arts David Talbot Rice CBE. A number of his friends and former pupils presented the University with works of art either from their personal collections or, in the case of practising artists, examples of their own work. This idea was conceived by Dr Harold Fletcher, who began the collection with the donation of a picture by John Houston which Professor Rice had once said he wished he could have bought for the University. Other artists featured include Elizabeth Blackadder, William MacTaggart, Mardi Barrie, Sam Bough and Anne Redpath.

David Talbot Rice was born in Gloucestershire in 1903 and attended Eton before studying archaeology and anthropology at Christ Church, Oxford, graduating in 1925. While in Oxford, his circle of friends included Evelyn

Pencil drawing of David Talbot Rice, by Emilio Coia

John Houston –
*Sea and Winter Sky*

Waugh and Harold Acton. The study of the art of Byzantium was one of his chief interests and he travelled extensively to pursue this, being involved in various expeditions to Cyprus, Asia Minor, Iraq and Iran. In 1932, Rice was appointed lecturer in Byzantine and Near Eastern Art at the newly founded Courtauld Institute in London. Then, in 1934, he was appointed to the Watson Gordon Chair of Fine Art at Edinburgh which he held until 1972, the year of his death. In 1975, the University's newly established Talbot Rice Gallery was named in his honour.

## THE COCKBURN GEOLOGICAL MUSEUM

The Cockburn Museum at King's Buildings holds an extensive collection of geological specimens and historical objects which reflect Edinburgh's prominent position within the geological sciences since the

Laboratory apparatus belonging to Sir James Hall of Dunglass, c. 1796–1820. James Hall is considered to be the founder of experimental geology

time of James Hutton (1726–97). The museum holds a number of collections of historical and research interest, many of which were donated in the late nineteenth and early twentieth centuries. These reflect the whole spectrum of Earth science materials – minerals, rocks, fossils – as well as maps, photographs and archives of activity by famous Earth scientists.

The collections have been housed at the Grant Institute since the building opened in 1932 and were largely catalogued and arranged during the early years of the Institute by Dr A. M. Cockburn. The considerable care, dedication and effort undertaken by Dr Cockburn on a voluntary basis led his colleagues to name the museum after him following his death in 1959. The original purpose of the museum dates back to 1873 when Professor Archibald Geikie, the holder of the first Chair of Geology at the University of Edinburgh, founded 'a museum for the teaching of geology', with the straightforward objective of having collections of minerals, rocks and fossils for the instruction of students. Geikie's example has been followed by many geological staff in the University, and the teaching collections have been continually added to. The huge expansion in both undergraduate and graduate student numbers in geology in the second half of the twentieth century is now supported by a much expanded teaching and research collection in the Cockburn Museum.

In addition to donations from staff and students, the existence of the museum over many years has led to major donations of special and rare specimens, particularly minerals. These provide extremely valuable reference material for research investigations as well as some beautiful specimens for display.

The Museum holds several collections and items of particular interest. These include:

- *Hall Collection*: collection of the first experimental apparatus for simulating melting and other processes in rocks: donated by Sir James Hall of Dunglass (1761–1832), a friend of James Hutton.

- *Brown of Lanfine Collection*: largely minerals donated by Dr Thomas Brown of Waterhaughs and Lanfine, 1874.
- *Jehu-Campbell Collection*: a collection of Highland Border Fossils, 1917–18: donated by Thomas James Jehu.
- *Lyell Rock, Mineral and Fossil Collection*: donated by Sir Charles Lyell, 1927.
- *Currie Mineral Collection*: a particularly fine collection donated by Dr James Currie, 1931.
- *Davidson Mineral Collection*: donated by James Davidson of Summerville, Dumfries, 1947.

Material in the Museum is used by staff and students but is also made available to visiting researchers, with individual items continuing to provide a vital resource many years after they were first collected.

## THE NATURAL HISTORY COLLECTIONS

The University has long had a 'museum' of natural history specimens, and the current incarnation of the Natural History Collections (NHC), in the Ashworth Laboratories at the King's Buildings, is a lively and well-used resource including nearly 30,000 individual

These Victorian lantern slides form part of the Natural History Collections

specimens, from skeletons and stuffed animals to parasitic organisms fixed on microscope slides. The collections have been built up over four centuries through the work of a line of curators aided by generous donations from private and public sources. In 1692, Robert Sibbald, Edinburgh's first professor of medicine, presented his collection of natural history specimens, and these formed the heart of the initial collection. The NHC grew from this generous donation and were the original occupants of the Old College quadrangle exhibition space that now houses the University's Talbot Rice Gallery. With the move to the King's Buildings site in the 1920s, a new custom home for the NHC was built.

One key role for the NHC since its inception has been to teach students about the diversity and structure of life. The collections provide the hundreds of specimens that students study from their first year, and are also used for thesis research by students at honours level. They are regularly visited by zoologists and other biological researchers especially interested in the older and rarer specimens. The collections are also used extensively by students from Edinburgh College of Art for research and inspiration. The NHC is involved in outreach to the public, with a 'treasure chest' of iconic specimens (such as skulls with very impressive teeth) taken to primary schools across Edinburgh, and the collections themselves open to the public on Doors Open Day each year, an event that includes demonstrations and hands-on exhibits. The NHC is also a registered museum, and holds nationally and internationally important collections, often related to the work of researchers within the University. There are, for example, major reference collections from the Australian Barrier Reef (the University led the first major research cruise to the reef in the 1930s) and from groups working to combat the scourges of insect-transmitted parasites in Africa.

## ANATOMY MUSEUM

As noted in Chapter 3, an 'Anatomical Museum' was to be an integral part of the new buildings when the architectural competition for premises for the medical school was announced in 1874. R. Rowand Anderson designed a top-lit galleried hall over three storeys, big enough to accommodate the skeletons of whales and dolphins, which

were suspended from the ceiling. With changes to pedagogic styles and decreasing reliance on specimens as a teaching aid, the museum was sub-divided in the 1950s and many of the non-human specimens were transferred to other museums – some of the whales are now on display in the Royal Museum of Scotland, where they are more publicly accessible. The museum contains many treasures and curiosities, including what must be the most grisly of 'bequests' ever made.

William Burke and William Hare were Irish labourers who arrived in Edinburgh in 1828 to work on the Union Canal, but who soon turned to murder as a more lucrative trade. At this time, medical schools were reliant on a supply of cadavers for dissection, and had traditionally been provided with the bodies of criminals who had been executed. However, as imprisonment rather than execution was increasingly used as a punishment, the supply dwindled. Bodysnatchers, or 'resurrectionists', exhumed the recently deceased and delivered them to the anatomists. Burke and Hare, however, famously turned

The anatomical museum, seen here in 1898, was at the heart of the new medical school which opened in 1884

to murder instead, delivering sixteen victims for dissection before being caught and charged. Burke was convicted; Hare turned King's evidence and escaped the death sentence, eventually making his way back to Ireland. In passing the death sentence on Burke, the Lord Justice-Clerk, David Boyle, took the view that mere execution would be inadequate punishment in a case as horrendous as this, and pronounced:

> I am disposed to agree that your sentence shall be put in execution in the usual way, but accompanied with the statutory attendant of the punishment of the crime of murder, viz. – that your body should be publicly dissected and anatomized. And I trust, that if it is ever customary to preserve skeletons, yours will be preserved, in order that posterity may keep in remembrance of your atrocious crimes.

Burke's body was indeed publicly dissected, with crowds of people attending. Members of the Edinburgh Phrenological Society were allowed to examine his skull. Burke's skeleton is on display in the Anatomy Museum, as are a number of life-masks and death-masks loaned to the University through the Ramsay Henderson Trust and the Phrenological Society.

Crowds turned out to witness the execution of William Burke on 28 January 1829

# 7

## Sports and
## Sporting Excellence

S PORT HAS BECOME SUCH a recognised and integral part of the university experience for many students that it is difficult to imagine that the development of organised sport is relatively recent in the long history of the University of Edinburgh, commencing properly only in the latter stages of the nineteenth century. This chapter charts the development of sports at the University, focusing on the philanthropic activities, giving, people, programmes and places which have made possible some notable successes.

The Centre for Sport and Exercise relaunched their climbing wall in 2014

INFORMAL GAMES

There are some records of physical games and activities being played at the University from its earliest days: in 1591, for example, only seven years after its foundation, the University was allotted its own playing field on the Burgh Muir, which was used on official 'play days' when students were taken to the field for a period of supervised games. In 1596, the town council also helped erect a 'catchpul' court inside the precincts of the University, a term which may have covered both rackets and tennis courts. Over the next four centuries – and in particular in the twentieth century – the development of sports grew and changed hugely, both in terms of facilities, offerings, programmes, widening access, and recognised value and importance, to become the integral and highly developed part of the university and student experience that it is today.

It is possible that the allocation of the Burgh Muir, an extensive area to the south of the city (now covered by the modern districts of Marchmont, Bruntsfield and Morningside) was done at least partly as a 'defensive' measure. There are many indications that students were unruly, with ball games and stone-throwing rife, several references to quite vicious snowball fights and even the occasional riot. The town council tried at various stages to impose discipline, but with little success. On the other hand, trying to contain large numbers of teenage boys during long days of study was always bound to be difficult, and

The Centre for Sport and Exercise provides facilities for a wide range of sport and exercise

Fitness advice is also available

the importance of providing space for legitimate exercise may have led to the provision of the first playing fields.

Archibald Flint, a student at the University in the seventeenth century, adorned his lecture notes with many illustrations. The borders and large initial capitals depict games of shooting, billiards, a type of tennis, a type of football and archery.

### EARLY YEARS: THE DETERMINATION OF STUDENTS

In 1866, the University Athletic Club was set up, which became the coordinating organisation for all sports clubs. The impetus for this came from students, who organised the first meeting to discuss the foundation of such a club on 9 May 1866, inspired by the practices at the universities of Oxford and Cambridge. Many of the students who were behind this push for the establishment of an organising body for sport came from local Edinburgh schools, such as the Edinburgh Academy, which had had a sports fiwweld since the 1850s. The students also received help from the University Senatus, in particular from two of its members, Professor Robert Christison and Sir Douglas Maclagan. The University's first athletics champion, in 1865, was C. R. Bauchope.

The development of sport in these early years was limited by lack of facilities: the new Athletic Club had no sports grounds, although

C. R. Bauchope

The University football team,
1877–8 (left) and the University
rugby team, 1882–3

it did have a gymnasium. The procurement of grounds was thus its first priority, and eventually in 1873 a field at Corstorphine was acquired for the Club with great help from Dr C. W. Cathcart, one of the Club's early members. Cathcart worked as a doctor in Edinburgh, played rugby for Scotland (1872–3) and was 'one of the most devoted members the Athletic Club has ever had'.

The first sport events held in June 1866 were a swimming match at Chain Pier, Trinity which was open to members of the Edinburgh University Athletic Club and a University Sports Day at Greenhill Park. The Athletic Club naturally encouraged interest and participation in field sports but also worked as the coordinating organisation for clubs for individual sports. These began to make their appearance from the 1870s onwards and members were a mixture of staff, students and graduates. Rugby was the most popular and prestigious sport at the time and an official club was established in 1871, followed by football, cricket, cycling, rowing and a variety of others. Arthur Conan Doyle's 1890 novel *The Firm of Girdlestone* gives a fictional account of life as a sports-playing student at Edinburgh at this time. Conan Doyle had

studied medicine at the University, graduating in 1881. He was a keen sportsman, and made the hero of his novel an Edinburgh student more focused on his rugby playing than his studies. Student clubs started emerging around 1900.

A row of early trophies

~

SPORTS FOR WOMEN

From 1892, women were admitted to study for degrees at the University. The foundation of various social and recreational clubs for women followed, as most existing student societies and clubs remained men-only, among them sports clubs. A women's cycling club and women's hockey club were pioneers in this regard, established in the last few years of the nineteenth century. In 1900, the Edinburgh Women Students' Athletic Club was formed, with the aim to 'promote physical exercise among women students'. At one of its first meetings, a committee member explained why she believed sports were important:

> I feel certain that when you have had a season's experience enjoying a healthy game in a piece of open country with a distant view of the Fife coast to the North, and our beloved city to the South of you, on any or every forenoon or afternoon of the week that you care to seek it, you will know that membership of an Athletic Club is a treasure worth paying for.

As had been the case with sports for men, access to grounds was a particular problem in the early years of women's athletics. The search for suitable grounds was made more difficult by the added requirement for 'privacy and protection from public gaze'. A field was eventually found and rented (at Windlestrawlee, Wardie Avenue), with the valuable support of individuals such as Douglas Chalmers Watson and his wife Alexandra Mary Campbell Geddes (who was

the first female medical graduate at Edinburgh in 1898). Douglas
Watson 'most generously subscribed to the rent and allowed his name
to be used as one of the guarantors' and Alexandra became the first
Honorary President of the Edinburgh Women's Athletic Club in 1920.
Hockey was by far the most popular sport among female students in
the early decades of the twentieth century.

The Women's Athletic Club joined forces with the Men's Athletic
Club to form Edinburgh University Sports Union in 1970.

### SPORTING GLORY: ERIC LIDDELL

One of the most famous sporting students of the University is
Eric Liddell, whose life and successes were immortalised by the
Oscar-winning 1981 film *Chariots of Fire*. Liddell was born in China,
the son of Scottish missionaries, and came to Edinburgh in 1920
to study for a BSc in Pure Science. He immediately became very
involved in sports, playing for the University rugby team as well as
joining the Athletic Club. He went to Paris for the 1924 Olympics as
part of the British athletics team and famously refused to participate
in his main event, the 100 metres, because the race series involved
competing on a Sunday and this conflicted with his religious beliefs.
He instead ran the 400 metres, a distance he was less familiar with,
and surprised everyone by not only winning the gold medal but also

setting a new world record of 47.6 seconds in the process. After his impressive performances in Paris (Liddell also won bronze in the 200 metres), he returned to Edinburgh to finish his degree. Eric Liddell was a multiple record holder in athletics (his British record for the 100 yards was unbeaten for thirty-five years) and also won seven international rugby caps for Scotland while at the University. He gained his University Blue in 1922.

In 1925, Liddell travelled back to China and worked as a missionary until his death in 1945. He was a strong believer in the value of sport as a means to promoting peace, solidarity and friendship and is said to have asserted at the University service after his graduation that 'in the dust of defeat as well as the laurels of victory, there is glory to be found if one has done his best'.

Eric Liddell's legacy lives on at the University through the Eric Liddell Gym, which originally opened in the Pleasance Sports Centre in 1981 before being relocated in 2010, and the Eric Liddell High Performance Sports Scholarships. These scholarships, launched to coincide with the start of the London 2012 Olympic Games, were set up in Liddell's honour as a way of ensuring that every student athlete is given the opportunity to achieve their full sporting potential. The scholarships are awarded to promising students to support their sporting development while studying, as the pressures in time and costs for those wishing to compete at the highest levels keep rising. Eric Liddell was the first athlete to be inducted into the University's Sports Hall of Fame when it was launched in 2008. A bronze statue of Liddell is on display in Old College.

Eric Liddell at the Paris Olympics in 1924

Liddell's medal is on display in the University

THINGS GET SERIOUS: THE ESTABLISHMENT
OF THE DEPARTMENT OF PHYSICAL EDUCATION

From those early years, opportunities to become involved with sports at the University continued to grow. New disciplines joined the list of existing sports clubs, as did many non-competitive activities such as hiking, skiing, cycling and camping. However, overall it was still a relatively small proportion of the student population which participated in these activities. In 1926, Lord Constable was invited by the University Court to form a special committee to 'consider and report on the questions generally of the Provision of Facilities for Student Athletic Activities and their Adequate Supervision'. His report made some far-sighted recommendations on how the University might better provide for sport and fitness. The Constable Report sowed the seeds of both the Department of Physical Education and the establishment of the Student Health Service at the University (the latter obviously predating the founding of the National Health Service). The report resulted in a new Athletics Committee, a Physical Welfare Fund in which a small levy was paid for each student and the appointment of a Director of Physical Training (the predecessor of today's Director of Sport and Exercise). The University thus realised the need to invest in the development of opportunities for sports and physical exercise as an enhancement of the student experience.

The first person to be appointed to the new post was Colonel Ronald Campbell, a former army gymnastics expert and Olympic fencer and boxer. He worked at Edinburgh from 1929 to 1946 and in this time he did much to encourage widening participation in sports and physical exercise. He had been very involved in the Boys' Club and Boy Scouts movements and believed exercise should be available to all. In these early stages he put much effort, for example, into making forms of exercise available which did not need expensive equipment,

Peter Heatly, 1955–6

Peter Heatly
*overleaf:* EDINBURGH UNIVERSITY SWIMMING TEAM, 1955–56
Scottish Universities Champions

instead favouring those which could involve many students at the same time. He also introduced the award of a physical education certificate in 1938, the Certificate of Physical Proficiency, which was the first of its kind in Britain. Colonel Campbell profoundly affected the development of sport at the University of Edinburgh. He heralded the transition of sports organisation from its amateur beginnings involving staff, students and graduates to an era of increasing professionalism and the recognition by the University of the importance of sports for all students. There have been six directors since Campbell's appointment in 1929; Jim Aitken is the current Director.

### Two case studies: C. W. Coghlan and J. J. M. Shaw

Dr Charles Wilfrid Coghlan won the University Heavy-weight Championship in 1909, beating the then-reigning star of Scottish boxing, David Revell Bedell-Sivright, also a graduate of Edinburgh. According to Usher, Coghlan 'was very tall and had a good boxing style, very upright and using his full height. He had a long hard punching straight left and had had experience in the English Championships'. Coghlan took the Triple Qualification in Medicine in 1902 and later practised as a doctor in Nottingham. On his death in 1937, Dr Coghlan left a bequest of £22,000 to the University for the development of the Athletic Club. He is thus an early example of the way in which the experience of sport at university can inspire people and encourage them to give something back to the organisation of sports which they enjoyed during their time as a student.

Many students who got involved with sport at the University have gone on to do great things: from achieving incredible sporting feats to giving back to the sporting clubs which they were part of, and so supporting the development of opportunities and access to sports for future generations. Of course, there are also cases of sporting characters going on to achieve great deeds in different fields. An example is John James McIntosh Shaw, who was captain of the Tennis Club in 1907, when the club was the second largest sports club at Edinburgh. Shaw was also (student) president of the Athletic Club in 1909 and president of the University Union, as well as holding a commission in the University's Officers' Training Corps. He studied medicine at the University and after graduation served in the Medical Corps during the First World War, receiving both the Military Cross and the French Croix de Guerre. He became an expert in plastic surgery and also founded the Edinburgh and East of Scotland Cancer Control Organisation. He returned to the University to serve as Rector's Assessor. In 1960, the Cancer Control Organisation for Edinburgh and South-East Scotland donated money to the University for research into the causes and treatment of the disease, including the provision of fellowships and travelling scholarships for this purpose. The fund was named the J. J. M. Shaw Cancer Research Fund.

### SIR DONALD POLLOCK: GREATEST BENEFACTOR

Many people have given their time, money and energy to support the growth of sports at the University over the years, but none have done more than John Donald Pollock. While a student at Edinburgh, Pollock played for the rugby and cricket teams. Sir Donald, as he was later known, continued his connections with the University long after his graduation. He had studied medicine at the University, graduating in 1895, after which he built up an illustrious career in medicine before moving on to work in the steel industry. He was elected Rector of the University from 1939 to 1945, and in 1945 he became the Honorary President of the Edinburgh University Athletic Club.

According to Usher, Sir Donald was 'probably the greatest single benefactor that the University has ever known'. He made a number of generous donations to the University, including the gift in 1942–3

The Pollock Gym was pressed into service for other uses during the Second World War and reopened in 1946

of the land and initial construction of the halls of residence complex which now bears his name. He also donated the Pleasance building to the University in 1938. The Pleasance complex is an iconic building which had previously been a beer brewer's workshop, and was transformed to provide a gym and other meeting space for the University's sports clubs. The new Pollock Gymnasium was reopened in 1946, having been used for other purposes during the Second World War in support of the nation's war effort. The building has undergone numerous transformations and expansions over the decades, becoming the first-class sporting facility which it is today.

And this is not all: in 1936, Sir Donald set up a trust in his name to support educational and religious activities in Scotland, making special reference to the University of Edinburgh and to the promotion of the welfare of its students. After his death in 1962, a second testamentary trust was set up to support these goals, and over the decades these trusts have continued to provide vital and generous support to the University, with a number of projects usually receiving funding every year. A large portion of this has been awarded to the development of sporting facilities at the University, in a bid to encourage in this way both access to and participation in sports and physical exercise among all students. Recent examples of projects made possible through the Pollock Trusts include the development of indoor climbing facilities in 2008 and 2014, five-a-side football courts in 2012, an outdoor archery pavilion in 2008, the dance studio in 2010, improved changing facilities in 2007 and 2009, and a bike park in 2009.

## PEFFERMILL: CHANGES OVER TIME

A great illustration of the changes which philanthropic giving has enabled to the development of sport at the University are the Peffermill playing fields. These fields were originally bought for the Women's Athletics Club in 1930, with help from the University Treasury as well as the Carnegie Trust for the Universities of Scotland. The land was originally laid out with a lacrosse pitch and three hockey pitches and provided the Women's Athletic Club with a focal point which became the centre of much of its activity.

The Peffermill playing field remained in use throughout the decades and is a prime example of the way in which facilities have

The women's fencing team, 1940–1

evolved and adapted to the changing needs of sporting students of the time. In 1986, for example, a first generation Astroturf artificial grass pitch was laid down – a huge stepping stone and an example of the University embracing new technology to revolutionise its sporting facilities. A clubhouse, with changing rooms and social facilities, was also constructed as a central hub for sports teams at Peffermill, and was named in honour of the then Director of Physical Education, Laurie Liddell.

In 2000, and with the help of a grant of £1.6 million from the National Lottery Sports Fund (the largest award of its kind at the time), Peffermill benefited from a further £3.5 million investment to create

Hockey at Peffermill in the 1970s

a world-class hockey training and competition centre. This is now a top-quality venue for student clubs, community users, national squads and the staging of major sporting events.

Peffermill has developed even further in recent years, commanding an enviable reputation nationwide as a location for big sporting events as well as inter-university and local competitions and for University club training. In 2013, the Peffermill playing fields received another upgrade as a new 3G pitch was unveiled; this new synthetic surface makes it possible to play in all weather conditions, a necessity for serious performance athletes who need to be able to train all year round. The new pitch was partly funded by the Scottish Government, through the CashBack for Communities programme. This programme reinvests the money seized from criminals through the Proceeds of Crime Act in programmes which will benefit Scotland's young people and their communities. As Justice Secretary Kenny MacAskill said:

> The 3G pitch at Peffermill is a fantastic example of the benefits our CashBack programme is bringing to communities in Edinburgh and elsewhere in Scotland. This state-of-the-art facility will allow local young people as well as grass roots rugby and football players to train in all weathers and hopefully help unearth some future sporting stars, especially with the Commonwealth Games only a year away.

The University of Edinburgh aims to give students a broad educational experience of sport: from gaining experience administrating a club, high-performance competition, to community participation and intra-mural social sports. Peffermill, which was originally bought with the aid of a philanthropic donation, has provided students with these types of experience over the years, and is an example of the way in which the University has adapted its sports offerings to fit the needs of the students. The Peffermill example also illustrates how it is necessary to evolve and upgrade sporting facilities continually in order to remain relevant, and shows the role philanthropic giving from a wide range of sources has played in achieving this.

## THE 1960S AND 1970S AND BEYOND: THE IMPACT OF PROFESSIONALISATION

In the 1960s and 1970s, the increasing professionalisation of sport had a significant impact on university sports too. As the divide between the demands for professional performance sport and amateur social sport grew, sports provision at the University had to adapt to reflect this change. The University had to ensure it continued to have the space and provisions to encourage as large a number of students as possible to participate in sport – at whatever level – while at the same

The merger with Moray House brought further academic developments to sports

Technology and performance swimming

The early tradition of fencing continues

time making sure it could provide the facilities necessary for aspiring professional athletes to develop their skills.

Again, philanthropic giving played a central role in this transitional period. Examples include bequests and donations of £500,000 for the sports hall and over £1 million for relocation of the Societies Centre from Hill Place to the Pleasance. A further major initiative saw the launch of FASIC (the Fitness and Sports Injury Clinic), providing a service to the University and the wider community. FASIC is now one of Scotland's leading and largest sports medicine providers.

The University's merger with Moray House College of Education in 1998 brought about the first professorial posts in sport, and introduced a tranche of sports-related students to the University, underpinning the latter's commitment to sport for students and its status in fuelling the sport and fitness industry. The Holyrood site provides an academic base for teaching and research programmes in physical education, sports science and recreation management.

## THINKING OUTSIDE THE GYM:
### FIRBUSH AND OUTDOOR EDUCATION

Outdoor activities had a history of popularity at the University of Edinburgh but it was only in the 1960s and 1970s that this developed significantly, as part of a new movement known as 'outdoor education'. The first training courses in outdoor education in Scottish colleges were established in 1973 at Moray House College and Dunfermline College (which were later to merge with the University). Edinburgh was a pioneer in the field of provision for outdoor education; in 1967, it opened the first purpose-built university outdoor education centre in the UK. Lord John Cameron, an Edinburgh judge who served on the University's legal team, provided much support to the project and was instrumental in persuading the McNab clan to sell the land

An early view of Firbush

A variety of ways of getting wet at Firbush

necessary for the project at Firbush on Loch Tay to the University. Lord Cameron, an Edinburgh graduate who had served as President of the Sports Union during his student years, contributed greatly to sport development, and Firbush was 'the jewel in the crown' of the then sports department: 'a great opportunity taken by the University at the time'. The boathouse was funded by Lord Balerno, and conversion of a basement room to a meeting room and social space was partially funded by Dr A. Sindison. Firbush has throughout the decades allowed students not only to discover a whole new range of sporting and physical exercise activities, but also to experience the glorious nature of Scotland. From its stunning surroundings on the shore of Loch Tay, it is also used as a venue for reading parties and is a popular destination for University families during its 'summer activity weeks', exposing the next generation to the challenges of orienteering and abseiling, and to the joys of getting wet in a variety of ways.

## SUCCESS STORIES AND THE HALL OF FAME

The University introduced its Sports Hall of Fame just before the 2008 Beijing Olympics to recognise and celebrate those students and staff who have achieved success on the world sporting stage. Induction into the Hall is the highest sporting honour the University can bestow, and the Hall of Fame serves as a real inspiration to the current

The Sports Hall of Fame honours staff and students

student community. Awards are made at the annual Blues and Colours Awards Ceremony, with the installation of a citation board which is on permanent display. These citation boards are a constant reminder of the sporting prowess of many students and graduates. Olympic champions Eric Liddell, Katherine Grainger and Sir Chris Hoy were amongst the first to join the Hall of Fame, which is now decorated by over twenty athletes across fourteen sports – with the number growing year on year.

Katherine Grainger in the gym which bears her name

GIVING BACK

As described above, the University has benefited hugely from philanthropic giving since the development of organised sports in the late
nineteenth century. This has helped it establish world-class sporting
facilities, giving students the opportunity to enhance their university
life and their education through participation in all kinds of sporting activities. Many of the students who have benefited from these
opportunities have decided to give something back, either to the
University or to the local community, as a way of expressing their
thanks. As an example, the University's Sports Union, in partnership
with the Active Schools network, has developed a community outreach programme in order to engage with and give back to the local
community of Edinburgh. The Friday Outreach programme provides
access to sport for schoolchildren in the Edinburgh area at the University's Peffermill playing fields, with training and coaching sessions
supported by students.

Sir Chris Hoy visiting the Eric Liddell
Gym in 2012

Another way in which former students have got involved with the University's constantly evolving sports development is through the Eric Liddell High Performance Scholarships. With the aid of donations from former students and well-wishers, these scholarships can be awarded annually. Supporters include two of the University's most illustrious sporting greats: cyclist and Olympian Sir Chris Hoy and Olympic rower Katherine Grainger are both patrons of the Eric Liddell Scholarship programme. As their foreword to the Scholarships brochure says:

> As Edinburgh graduates, we know first-hand the time given over to our respective sports and the difficulties of juggling studies with competing at a world class level. As students, we would get up in the early hours of the morning for training, attend lectures and then return to training in the evening. Doing a part-time job was just not possible and luckily the support we received meant we did not have to. This support made our eight Olympic medals possible. It is now time for us to look to our current and future student athletes who have the potential to go on and achieve greatness on the world sporting stage … We hope, through the establishment of the Eric Liddell High Performance Sports Scholarships, we can ensure that future generations of University athletes get their chance to shine.

An example of a student who has benefited from this scholarship programme is Sarah Robertson, a second-year law student and talented hockey player. Sarah was recently chosen to be part of the GB Youth Olympic Squad, competing in the 2013 Youth Olympics in Australia, where the squad won bronze. She was also a central member of the University's women's hockey team that claimed the British Universities & Colleges Sport (BUCS) Trophy, and she continues as a rising star in the women's national squad that is focusing on the 2014 Commonwealth Games in Glasgow. Sarah was awarded the Captain S. T. Garner Trophy in 2013 for the most outstanding contribution to University sport by a first-year student, and has received an Eric Liddell High Performance Sports Scholarship. She comments: 'It's not just the financial support that's important, but the recognition that comes with being awarded a scholarship like this. In terms of academic flexibility the University is incredibly accommodating, especially with those awarded the Eric Liddell Scholarships'.

Sarah Robertson receiving the Eric Liddell Scholarship in 2012, with Katherine Grainger and HRH The Princess Royal

In addition to the Eric Liddell Scholarship, and thanks to generous donations by University alumni, the University is now able to offer a suite of tailored sports bursaries and scholarships for talented student athletes. These include the Katherine Grainger Scholarship for Sporting Excellence (established in 2012, multi-sport), the MacAskill Family Elite Sport Bursary (2013, multi-sport) and the David Bedell-Sivright Performance Sport Bursary (2014, rugby).

# 8

## Student Life

THE PREVIOUS CHAPTER explored the sporting life of the University and the ways in which philanthropy has enabled students to develop themselves whilst also competing at local, national and international level in numerous activities. This chapter looks at other aspects of student life in Edinburgh, and how the student experience has been enhanced over the years by many developments, some of which were world-leading in their time. The generosity of sponsors helped deliver the earliest student accommodation, and other 'pump-priming' initiatives led to students developing other ventures which continue to benefit students today. Just as philanthropy helps the students and their experience, students 'give' to the University and the community using their time and expertise.

International students model the University's new tartan on St Andrew's Day, 2007

THE FOUNDATION OF THE UNION

All students are automatically members of the Edinburgh University Students' Association (EUSA), and Edinburgh boasts the oldest Student Union in the UK. The Students' Representative Council (SRC) was founded in 1884 by Robert Fitzroy Bell. Shortly after its foundation, the SRC agreed to the formation of a Union in order to provide a meeting place for all students from all faculties. This building is known today as Teviot Row House. An excellent account of the foundation of the Union is contained in *No Spirits and Precious Few Women: Edinburgh University Union 1889–1989*, edited by Iain Catto, from which the extracts below are taken. One of the Union's first Honorary Life Members, Professor S. H. Butcher, described the purpose of the Union as:

> The idea of the Union as it existed in the minds of its founders, and as it still exists in our own mind is that it should be the focus of the collective life of students – the centre of every social interest and intellectual activity; the meeting place of all faculties and all societies; the arena of debating and discussion, where young orators may display their powers of speech and prepare themselves for the world … Speaking generally, our idea is to perfect the Union as an instrument of social intercourse and of human fellowship to bring into it a greater diversity of elements, to add everything that can enrich and invigorate the young life of its members, that can relieve the monotony of toil, and that can dignify amusement, and so contribute to the refined enjoyment of all students during their University career.

In 1884, the University's Chancellor, Lord President Inglis, was tasked to undertake the necessary fundraising for the construction of a Union building. Letters were sent out to prominent men and public subscription lists were opened up. Contributions included large sums from the University Senatus and the Edinburgh town council, with the greatest contribution coming from the proceeds of the Edinburgh University Union Fancy Fair. The Fancy Fair was held on the Edinburgh Waverley Market site over four days:

> The greatest contribution made to the funds was to be the Fancy Fair held on the site of Waverley Market from Tuesday November 30 to Saturday December 4. Each day the Fair was opened at noon by a distinguished guest and continued with a variety of entertainments and attractive stall until 9.30 pm at night. A theatrical performance of Punch

The Fancy Fair in 1886 raised £10,000 towards Teviot House

and Judy was performed twice daily, and there were exhibitions of scientific experiments, optical experiments and a magic lantern exhibition of photographs from the Old Masters. Regimental Bands, concerts and theatricals helped to keep the crowds amused, and the large range of stalls relieved them of their money. The Royal Company of Archers' Stall contained a Wheel of Fortune, curiosities from India, Madeira and Japan and Edelweiss pottery; the Royal Infirmary Ward Stall presented Bulgarian embroideries, tiger and leopard skins and Japanese metalwork; and the Law Stall had on display Moorish woodwork, Gibraltar pottery and Bavarian stools. These were but a mere selection of the delightful articles on display. All the stall-holders were in costume, from those from Erin's Isle in Irish Costume to those on the Indian Stall in turbans and veils. Refreshments were sumptuously provided, at a charge naturally, and a variety of amusements, from shooting galleries to a race table, were designed to attract the visitor in the Country Fair. The Stewards of the Fair were all elegantly costumed in sixteenth century period costume. The whole Fair was organised by a Committee of Management, comprising [James Avon] Clyde and [Robert Fitzroy] Bell, Archibald Fleming (the then President of the SRC), Professor Cossar Ewart, W A Wood CA as Treasurer, and Mrs C W Cathcart, who acted as Honorary Secretary of the Ladies Committee, and played a formidable role in the success of the Fair, through her recruitment of many of the ladies of Edinburgh Society, plus HRH The Princess Christian and HRH the Duchess of Edinburgh as Patronesses. It is noteworthy that the part played in the success of the Fair by the ladies was equal to that of the gentlemen.

Each day the *Journal of the Fair* was published and at 3d a copy, sold exceedingly well. A further publication at the Fair also proved extremely successful. This was *The New Amphion*, published on St Andrews Day 1886. It was an anthology of verse and prose in a dainty little pocket-sized volume, with contributions from amongst others, Robert Browning, Robert Louis Stevenson and John Stuart Blackie. It was in fact rather a remarkable literary event in its own accord.

The Fair averaged some 8000 visitors each day, and it raised some £10,000 towards the cost of building the Union.

The Edinburgh University Union Fancy Fair in 1886, with its accompanying book of literary lollipops *The New Amphion*, was probably the first example of a tie-in publication as a fundraiser, and it gave rise to others in the University. The idea was subsequently copied at other universities. Edinburgh publications included *Field Bazaar*, published in 1896 to raise funds for a pavilion on the University playing field, accompanied by a special Bazaar number of *The Student* magazine to which Arthur Conan Doyle (later Sir Arthur) contributed a specially written Sherlock Holmes short story, *The Memoirs of*

*Sherlock Holmes – The Field Bazaar*. A society bazaar was held in 1907 in the Music Room in the Assembly Rooms in George Street to raise funds for premises for the Edinburgh Indian Association which, it was hoped, would match those of the well-established South African Union, which was in existence from 1881 to 1939.

*The New Amphion*

In 1889 a Begging Committee was appointed by the SRC to raise the final funds needed to open the building, and the Edinburgh University Union opened its doors on Saturday, 19 October 1889. Student member subscription at the time was half a guinea and graduates could subscribe as a life member for five guineas.

The title of the Union's centenary booklet, *No Spirits and Precious Few Women: Edinburgh University Union 1889–1989*, was a reference to the fact that spirits were not sold in the Union bar until 1970, and that women were only allowed into certain areas of the Union as guests, even after women were admitted to the University as students. The Edinburgh University Women's Union was founded in 1906, remaining in existence until 1964, when it became the Chambers Street Union.

The Women's Union in George Square (left) and the Men's Union in Teviot House, in the late 1940s

Teviot Row House, around 1905

Teviot Row House has undergone many changes through the years and in 1971 was officially listed as a building of special architectural and historic interest. This was the same year that the Union opened its doors to female members. The minute book at the time explains that a group of women invaded the Smoking Room of the Union on 13 January 1970. Following debate of this issue at the Committee of Management meeting later that month to make sure this did not happen again, it was agreed that 'the Doorman should keep his eyes open for large numbers of women'.

The Students' Association was formed in 1973, bringing together four Unions, the Societies Council and the Students' Representative Council to provide amenities, representation and facilities for all

Teviot Row House and the McEwan Hall, 1897

students. A Committee of Management-elect was formed in May 1973, at which the formation of bye-laws was initially discussed.

Today the Student Union provides services to students across its four buildings: Teviot Row House, Potterrow, the Pleasance and King's Buildings House.

### POLLOCK HALLS OF RESIDENCE

As noted in Chapter 2, Edinburgh never became a truly residential university on the model of Oxford or Cambridge, and students historically lived with their families or in privately rented lodgings. There were suggestions that these arrangements were in part to blame for the poor levels of discipline – which exercised both the University and the town council on many occasions as they tried to regulate student behaviour by outlawing certain activities or by, for example, putting public houses out of bounds. With no provision for meals in the college, however, students were able to argue that they visited taverns not to drink, but to buy a midday meal. During the 1830s and 1840s, and particularly in 1838, snowball riots took place; in 1838 thirty-five students were arrested and charged with 'mobbing, rioting and assault' after a fracas between them and some workmen; police were involved and the Lord Provost summoned soldiers from the Castle. As time went by, the appeal of having spaces in which to socialise with other students outside study-time is evident in the foundation of the Union, and discipline seems to have improved markedly thereafter.

Chancellor's Court at Pollock Halls, opened in 2003

St Leonard's House from printers' playing fields, now the site of the Commonwealth Pool

Sir Donald Pollock, by Stanley Cursiter

Students did not want to simply return to their lodgings in the evenings and 'in 1876, fifty students assembled at 54 South Bridge in order to establish a Students' Club "to afford special advantages for students residing in lodgings, who prefer to dine together at moderate rates" … Within six months there were some 450 members with 200 dining daily'. But perhaps underlying this enthusiasm for extending the times at which students communed was a desire to create a large-scale alternative to the lodgings to which Student Club members would have returned after their famed dinners.

Set in an unforgettable location at the foot of Arthur's Seat, yet only a short walk away from the University's George Square campus, it is difficult to imagine the University of Edinburgh without Pollock Halls of Residence. The area appears on record as early as 1261 following the foundation of St Leonard's Hospital and Chapel. Several impressive buildings were constructed in the following years and are now part of the complex. An Edinburgh merchant named Alexander Scott built the Salisbury Green mansion in the 1750s, now in use as hotel-quality guest and meeting accommodation. In 1869, the publisher Thomas Nelson built St Leonard's Hall nearby. From 1925 until 1939, St Leonard's was the home of St Trinnean's Girls School, rumoured to have inspired Ronald Searle's cartoon, *St Trinian's*.

The bringing together of the buildings in the area as a multi-building halls of residence is attributable to the generosity of Sir Donald Pollock. By the time his three-year tenure as Rector ended in 1942, Pollock had acquired the estate from the Nelson family, who had owned much of it previously, and donated it to the University. Pollock's distinguished career was even more varied than the description given in an article in the *Glasgow Herald* following his death at the age of ninety-four in 1962, which described him as a 'physician, business man, and philanthropist'. After studying at Glasgow and Edinburgh, the Galashiels-born baronet

(as of 1939) worked as a ship's doctor prior to setting up a practice in London. He was subsequently chairman of British Oxygen from 1932 to 1939, having purchased the patent to a form of liquid oxygen.

Detail from the staircase at St Leonard's House

Sir Thomas Holland

Although some students moved into Salisbury Green and St Leonard's immediately after the Second World War it was not until the 1960s that new buildings were designed to meet the growing demand for student housing. When the first, Holland House, was built in 1960, it set a precedent in being named after a person who had performed a notable service to the University – in this case, Sir Thomas Holland, who had been Principal and Vice-Chancellor of the University from 1929 to 1944.

~

### MASSON HALL

The name 'Masson' has featured multiple times in the names of Edinburgh student accommodation. In 1994, a 133-person Masson House was built within the grounds of Pollock Halls of Residence. It replaced Masson Hall, a smaller residence that had sat at South Lauder Road since 1965. Arguably the most pivotal Masson residence, however, was the Masson Hall established at 31 George Square in 1897, the foundation of which was embedded within the struggle for women's suffrage.

David Mavor Masson, painted by
Sir George Reid

From 1867, the Edinburgh Ladies Educational Association (ELEA, later known as the Edinburgh Association for the University Education of Women – EAUEW) campaigned for the improvement of education for women. Luminaries such as the ELEA's secretary Mary Crudelius (1839–77) and founding member of the Edinburgh Ladies' Debating Society Sarah Siddons Mair (1846–1941) had begun the movement by organising lectures for women at a time when they were not permitted to enrol officially at universities. One of the Edinburgh academics who helped the ELEA struggle for access to lectures was Aberdeen-born scholar David Masson (1822–1907), who was the Chair of Rhetoric and English Literature at the time. In January 1868, Masson began to teach for the EAUEW with a course in English literature for which 'over 400 ladies [attended] the first meeting, and 265 sign[ed] up for the [whole] course'. Professor Masson also supported Sophia Jex-Blake's contemporaneous campaign for women to have the right to study medicine at Edinburgh. Whilst this was not philanthropy in the financial sense, these changes could only happen through various people giving up their time to help women into education at the University.

After the EAUEW won their fight to have women's studies at the University accredited, members began to work to establish facilities for female students. Philanthropist and education campaigner Margaret Houldsworth (1839–1909) was particularly central to gathering funds for the foundation of a women's residence from sources including the Phoebe Blyth Library Gift and the Pfeiffer Trust. The success of their campaign enabled them to use 31 George Square as Masson Hall, so named after 'the ELEA's mentor and chief supporter'. The foundation of Masson Hall brought about the closure of a smaller residence for women, Crudelius Hall, which had been named after Professor David Masson's ally in the fight for educational equality at Edinburgh.

Sophia Jex-Blake was determined to study medicine and started campaigning to do so in 1869, eventually suing the University unsuccessfully. She moved to Berne to qualify. Largely as a result of her struggles, degrees for women were sanctioned by Act of Parliament in 1889

BEDLAM THEATRE AND THE EUTC

It is of little surprise that Edinburgh is a hub of artistic and literary activity outside the confines of the month of August, in which the city plays host to the world-famous Festival Fringe. What is striking, however, is the extent to which students have been – and continue to be – at the heart of Edinburgh's artistic life. One of the most visible hubs of Edinburgh students' artistic and performance efforts is Bedlam Theatre, the view of which meets all who walk down George IV Bridge from the direction of the Royal Mile. Run by the Edinburgh University Theatre Company (EUTC), Bedlam is the oldest student-run theatre in the United Kingdom.

George Square Gardens during the Edinburgh Festival Fringe

Bedlam Theatre

Admiring Bedlam's neo-gothic architecture, few would be surprised to learn that the building was first a church. In 1846, Glasgow-born architect Thomas Hamilton's design was erected as the New North Free Church. For some years it was used as the University's chaplaincy. However, when the EUTC chose a name for the building when they took it over in 1980, they drew inspiration from a now disbanded nearby building: the Edinburgh Bedlam Mental Institute.

The EUTC put on an average of forty plays each year, in addition to Friday night performances by the perennially popular improvised comedy troupe The Improverts. Since 1979, selected University buildings have been used as Edinburgh Festival Fringe venues. The connections between the University and the Fringe have no doubt contributed to the national and even international successes enjoyed by several productions that began in Bedlam. In 2008, *Eight*, which Edinburgh alumna Ella Hickson wrote, directed and put on at Bedlam with a cast of Edinburgh students, won the Carol

The Improverts

Tambor Best of Edinburgh Award, funding a run of the play in New York.

The Bedlam Youth Project works to help children and young people get more involved with Bedlam, offering them the opportunity to gain hands-on experience not only with acting, but with theatre administration, costumes and technical skills. This involves inviting children from Edinburgh schools to take part in plays and also holding workshops enabling children to access theatres who might not ordinarily have the opportunity.

## THE STUDENT

The first issue of *The Student*, 'the UK's first student newspaper', was printed in 1887. It was founded by Dundonian Robert Cochrane Buist (1860–1939), a man of exceptionally broad talent who later worked as a pioneering obstetrician and gynaecologist and was Chair of the Scottish Council of the British Medical Association. The establishment of *The Student* was considered to constitute 'the permanent interpreter of student opinion', which the founders contrasted to 'ephemeral periodicals such as the *Edinburgh University Magazine* of 1871, in which Robert Louis Stevenson first appeared in print'. After Buist's graduation in 1888, *The Student* was taken over by the Students' Representative Council, which had been founded four years earlier.

The first issue of *The Student* (1887)

An issue of *The Student* from 1955

Over the years *The Student* has, of course, gone through a good deal of adjustment to changing times and technologies: from a change of premises from the Student Publications Board to the Pleasance in the 1990s, to the introduction of computers to aid the production of the weekly newspaper. The manner in which it is funded has also changed: in 1992 *The Student* stopped being funded by the Student Union and instead carried on with a £5,000 grant from the University Development Fund. The newspaper had previously cost 30 pence, but the award allowed it to become free of charge.

*The Student*'s national excellence has been recognised by the awarding of an impressive list of prizes over the years, including *The Guardian*'s 'Best Newspaper on a Shoestring' in 2001. Buist set a precedent for *The Student* alumni going on to influential careers after graduation, including former Prime Minister Gordon Brown, who was news editor in the 1970s.

## EDINBURGH UNIVERSITY SETTLEMENT

There is a long tradition of Edinburgh students being involved with community matters, from assisting fellow students to helping people in Edinburgh outside the University, and indeed aiding those overseas. Some efforts seem rather specific to their time. One notable example from 1859 was the senior-professor-led University of Volunteers for Home Defence, a reaction to anxiety about the prospect of a French invasion. The Volunteers are reported as having 'drilled in the Old Quadrangle and skirmished over Arthur Seat [sic]'. Other charitable efforts might be seen instead as long-term projects and the result of a great deal of care and hard work by generations of Edinburgh students.

The Edinburgh University Settlement Association was founded in 1905 with the aim of bridging the divide between 'town and gown', particularly by alleviating the effects of poverty on the lives of less-privileged Edinburgh residents. The Settlement's first annual report tells of a successful series of springtime 'Saturday Night Concerts', with audiences of 170 per performance, for which the Settlement thanked the University Musical Society for their efforts; the

Newspaper coverage of Edinburgh University Settlement's Golden Jubilee in 1955

establishment of a 'Guild for Boys and Girls' where participants spent some of their time learning 'a Kinderspiel, which the children will sing to their parents and friends at the end of the winter'. A range of sporting activities – including a swimming club that met at the Corporation Baths situated on Infirmary Street and a football club that trained in Holyrood Park – appeared a particular note of pride at the time, so successful they 'proved a most valuable meeting-ground for members and students'. Although Edinburgh University Settlement was declared bankrupt in 2010, the charity's philosophy could be said to live on in the EUSA Volunteering Centre.

## CHILDREN'S HOLIDAY VENTURE

'All of our activities involve picking up the children, and providing care and play away from home. We don't have an educational mission, although good manners are nice. Play is a basic right, and we attempt to let kids be kids' – this is the philosophy that leads the work done by Children's Holiday Venture (CHV), which is not only Edinburgh students' longest-running – and no doubt most impactful – charitable organisation, but 'the oldest fully student run charity in the United Kingdom'.

Plans for an Edinburgh-based CHV group were started by graduate Martyn Edelsten, who had been inspired by the work of the Cambridge-run group Children's Relief International in Germany. In 1963, Edelsten took twenty-three children to the Black Forest in Germany. A report of the trip said that

> First, it gave the children a good holiday and we hope the parents a good rest. Secondly, it showed the children that somebody was prepared to take trouble over them and that they themselves could do quite a lot to help themselves. Thirdly it taught them to live with others because we enforced discipline … Lastly we hope that the camp will have stirred in them an interest in one or more hobbies, which they will now follow up, although back in conditions for the most part very unlike those of the camp … we thank them for making the camp a very rewarding experience for us.

After the Edinburgh chapter of the group was founded in 1964, its members decided to meet the need for better opportunities for those living in poverty closer to home. They turned their attention to the less privileged areas of Edinburgh, becoming independent of Children's Relief International in the process. From then on, CHV experimented with a range of holiday arrangements, from camping to youth hostelling. In time, holidays were coupled with non-residential activities for Scottish children, such as parties, day outings and fundraisers. Volunteers now organise weekly outings for groups of children (with groups comprising children aged 8–12 and 12–16). These trips include swimming and bowling, as well as craft nights. As a testament to the sustained dedication of Edinburgh students to working with local children, in 2013 many cohorts of CHV volunteers celebrated the group's fiftieth anniversary with a ball in Teviot.

## EUSA VOLUNTEERING CENTRE

With the University keen to make the most of students' enthusiasm for helping others by aiding them to find projects that matched their interests and timetables, 2010 marked the foundation of the EUSA Volunteering Centre. Situated at Connect in Potterrow, the aim of the Centre is to provide a welcoming and informative space for potential student volunteers. Popular projects on which to volunteer include Gorgie City Farm, South East Scotland Scouts and the Grassmarket Community Project. However, the Volunteering Centre also understands that many students keen to help out would like extra guidance in choosing a project so that they might find one where they can make as big a difference as possible. With this in mind, the Volunteering Centre's eVOLve weekly volunteering club gives students the opportunity to work on a different project each week, taking part in diverse initiatives such as 'beach clean ups, tree planting and helping at local primary schools'. Those who work at the Volunteering Centre and the volunteers themselves agree that one of the many positive aspects of volunteering through the University of Edinburgh is that it is popular with both UK and international students alike.

Contemporary volunteering work in which Edinburgh students participate is based on the

Students on a tour of volunteering projects during Freshers' Week

During the Freshers' Week Fair, students sign up for a variety of voluntary activities

philosophy that students have the power to make big differences in the lives of those around them. As the University becomes increasingly international, students become more and more enthusiastic to consider what can be done to make fellow students feel as valued and welcomed as possible whilst studying in Edinburgh. EUSA's peer-proofreading scheme is a remarkable example of a local, modest initiative making a huge difference to the experience of students whose first language is not English. The scheme is delivered by EUSA, with training for volunteers provided in collaboration with the Institute for Academic Development. Each year around fifty to sixty volunteers proofread in the region of 400 assignments for their international colleagues.

## 'STUDENTS IN THE COMMUNITY' NEIGHBOURHOOD PARTNERSHIP EVENT

EUSA representatives have maintained links with community stakeholders by holding an annual community event. The last three events have been held jointly with the City of Edinburgh Council's South Central Neighbourhood Partnership. These events have provided an opportunity for students and other local residents, community councils, University, police, youth forums, councillors, MSPs and city council staff to get together to discuss local issues and come up with projects to benefit the local area. The event helps students to find out more about their local area, helps other community members find out about the good things that students already contribute to the area and promotes opportunities for students and non-students to work together.

The Neighbourhood Partnership has a Community Grant Fund for local projects and for this event it has previously dedicated up to

£6,000 for projects that students and community members bring as proposals. The kinds of projects that have been funded so far include:

- art workshops in local care homes run by a student art society
- creative writing workshops in a local community centre which resulted in a poetry publication
- a youth band night run by a local youth forum
- a space in a local students' union building for young people to socialise in during the evening
- a swap shop/freecycle initiative run by a student society – reusing unwanted items and running workshops for the community.

PEER SUPPORT

Peer Support at Edinburgh covers a wide range of projects, with the common aims of forming supportive academic communities and using the shared experiences of students to facilitate the learning, and personal and professional development, of their peers. A few pockets of good practice were previously scattered across the colleges, but since 2013 the Peer Support team at EUSA now supports all twenty-two schools of the University to develop new peer support schemes that will eventually be available to all students.

To cater for the broad variety of academic programmes across the University, extensive resources are produced for six basic models of peer support, from which each school customises its projects to suit its students. These range from school-wide 'house' systems (in which every student is assigned to a house with a dedicated support network of tutors and special socials and events) to mentoring and befriending schemes, academic families, helpdesks and peer-assisted learning schemes (PALS).

PALS is a specific model of peer learning that is very popular and widely applicable to many disciplines at different levels – from individual modules to whole degree programmes. More experienced students lead regularly scheduled voluntary sessions with small groups of new students. The sessions are based around course material with a focus on learning processes and study skills. As well as introducing collaborative and independent styles of learning, both first-year students and the student leaders facilitating the sessions have the opportunity to develop strong interpersonal professional skills and graduate attributes. PALS sessions also foster cross-year interaction and discussion and are great spaces in which to ask questions and try different ways of learning in a safe environment.

Peer Support began as a joint project between the University of Edinburgh and EUSA in September 2012 as a strand of Enhancing Student Support (ESS), with one staff member. The project had expanded to a team of two full-time and nine part-time staff by September 2014, and now reports through the Student Experience Project. The Peer Support team maintains good working relationships with the Institute of Academic Development (IAD) as well as academic, administrative and support staff, and students from all schools.

Embedded in EUSA's Representation and Student Support team, the Peer Support Project has a student-focused approach and collaborates with other central services to run programmes such as International Buddies (with EUSA Global team), a buddying scheme matching returning exchange students with visiting exchange students.

Cycling across the Meadows

# 9

# The Gift of Time
# and Expertise

WHILST THIS BOOK largely focuses on philanthropic gifts of money that have changed the University and enabled it to grow and develop, there is another kind of contribution – that of time, expertise, experience and networks. This could warrant another volume in itself but is briefly covered here to show the wide variety of activities which take place and their value to the University. In turn, the huge community of staff and students benefit the wider community, through involvement in activities not related directly to research and scholarship.

## CONTRIBUTING TO THE UNIVERSITY'S GOVERNANCE

Every university has a governing body; at Edinburgh this is the University Court. Members of Court are drawn from a range of backgrounds and donate their time and expertise to ensure the University is effectively run and complies with funding and government regulations. This group makes sure that the student voice is heard and that committees run effectively. Court also oversees the University's finance, remuneration, promotions and investments to ensure strategy is suitable for the sustainability of the University.

University Court members include assessors from the General Council, the Senatus (which is the body responsible for academic decision-making), the Provost of the City of Edinburgh, a student member and a non-teaching staff member. Crucially, the University is also supported by a number of members of Court who bring their

Rector Ian McWhirter being 'chaired' in 2009

expertise in accountancy, audit, business, education, investment and much more.

The four ancient Scottish universities each have a Rector, but their roles and appointment methods vary slightly. At Edinburgh, the post of Rector was created in the nineteenth century, and every three years, a Rector is elected by the students, staff and alumni – a feature unique to the University of Edinburgh. The Rector chairs the University Court, and thus makes a crucial input to the University's governance and strategic direction.

Edinburgh's Rectors have been an interesting mix of people. There have been future and serving politicians and military leaders including Gladstone, Lord Lothian, Field Marshal Lord Kitchener, David Lloyd George, Winston Churchill, Dr Gordon Brown, Sir David Steel and Tam Dalyell. Media celebrities have also featured, such as Magnus Magnusson and Muriel Gray. Sir Alexander Fleming, discoverer of penicillin, is the only scientist to have held the role. Sometimes battles are fought to win the role, and on other occasions a Rector is elected unopposed. Inevitably, some Rectors have been more actively involved than others and have made more of an impact. Several have been building a career while in the post, whilst others already had an established career and profile, and had proven expertise in their own domain. Many have been excellent for the University, supporting students effectively while also making a major contribution to strategy.

The Rector and members of Court sit on several University committees concerned primarily with the non-academic aspects of running a multi-million-pound enterprise – Estates, Health and Safety, Finance and General Purposes, Investment, Remuneration, Risk Management and Staff Committee. Their varied perspectives and external knowledge help the University to develop and deliver ambitions and goals.

Members of Court are also good ambassadors for the University. They may challenge University management frequently, but they also understand the issues and circumstances the University faces. As such, their advice is warmly welcomed and their experience in different walks of life is valued fully. They are seen as 'critical friends' to the University.

## GENERAL COUNCIL

The General Council consists of graduates, academic staff and members of the University Court. It has a statutory right to comment on matters which affect the well-being and prosperity of the University, with the aim of ensuring that graduates have a continuing voice in the management of its affairs. The General Council elects the University's Chancellor.

## THE CHANCELLOR

The Chancellor is the figurehead of the University. The holder of the position will come to key events like graduations, open buildings, talk and encourage staff when they hear about new projects and promote the value of the University by sharing their expertise and often their assets. The University's current Chancellor is HRH The Princess Royal who is an excellent committed ambassador, giving a lot of her time. She is very knowledgeable about many things and engages enthusiastically with staff, students and supporters. Previous holders of the title include the Earl of Balfour and the Marquis of Linlithgow, but a truly devoted Chancellor was HRH Prince Philip, Duke of Edinburgh, who held the position from 1953 to 2010.

The Duke of Edinburgh has been a regular visitor to the University over this long period. He has conferred many degrees on world leaders and opened his palaces for the University to thank its supporters, hosting many dinners at Holyrood and Buckingham Palace. His Royal Highness visited several times a year, and

HRH Prince Philip, Duke of Edinburgh, was inaugurated as Chancellor in 1953 and served until 2010

The Chancellor inspecting the Informatics Forum in August 2008

always selected a variety of things to review. Genuinely interested in education and new scientific advances, he kept everyone on their toes, asking insightful questions. He was keen to visit less visible projects, like those encouraging students from disadvantaged backgrounds to raise their aspirations, develop their skills and think about the value of higher education to their future. The Duke of Edinburgh opened many University buildings, a recent one being the Chancellor's Buildings named in his honour. Despite His Royal Highness supporting the University for almost sixty years, his enthusiasm for this role never tired.

## CAMPAIGN BOARDS

Numerous people support Campaign Boards, some for University-wide campaigns and some for specific projects and disciplines, and have helped to deliver huge change in the University. The most recent University-level Campaign Board supported the delivery of £350 million to enhance the capabilities of the University through a wide range of projects, some of which are covered elsewhere in this book.

## EMERITUS AND HONORARY PROFESSORS

Many professors when they retire are awarded the title of Professor Emeritus, and continue to help the University in many ways. Some continue to teach, while others do research and develop their disciplines, and provide advice to colleagues. Another crucial group are the honorary professors. There are currently over twenty honorary professors in the College of Humanities and Social Science, almost forty in the College of Science and Engineering and over sixty in the College of Medicine and Veterinary Medicine. Honorary professors are drawn from outside the University and bring an external perspective and expertise. They include clinicians working for the National Health Service who work in research and teaching in an honorary capacity, and business experts or politicians who give lectures and seminars and support students. Others contribute in an advisory capacity. All of these talented people have been giving their expertise freely to the University over many years and play a key part in the University's ability to offer such a diverse range of courses to students whilst remaining at the forefront of research and knowledge exchange.

## SUPPORTING STUDENTS IN DEVELOPING THEIR CAREERS

With an increasing emphasis on employment prospects for our graduates in a changing world and at a time of global economic uncertainties, the provision of internship opportunities and graduate traineeships is invaluable in preparing graduates for work in a way which will hopefully have a career-long impact. Mentoring and coaching opportunities, whether provided by individuals or businesses, are an excellent way of making a contribution. The impact of these initiatives can be far-reaching. In turn, those providing such opportunities often mention the benefits they and their businesses have derived from the fresh new perspective brought by a student or recent graduate – a true 'win-win' situation.

## ALUMNI AND FRIENDS WHO HELP
## IN THEIR AREA OF EXPERTISE

A large number of people contribute huge amounts of brainpower, time and energy. It is impossible to list here all the ways in which this happens, so the following are just a few examples.

### *Piers Sellers, astronaut*

One of the University's science alumni, Piers Sellers, took an unusual career route: he became an astronaut and took part in many space missions. He has supported the University in many ways, and has made a particularly valuable contribution in community engagement and outreach. One participant in an event Piers took part in – a talk for schools and the public – described the event in New College as follows:

> The stage was set up with big screens and many excited groups of young people were assembled. The lights went down and in walked Piers in his NASA astronaut suit with three of his Apollo colleagues. It was immediately total gasps and quiet. It was also a good balance for role models, two males and two females and one of the females was black. Between them they recounted the adventures of the mission, what it is like in

Astronaut Piers Sellers

space day to day and what they were studying and finding out about and how they each had a different job. Being able to see the earth from space, what it was physically like during take-off, and so much more. They answered many questions with humour and ease. They finished by telling the largely young audience how crucial it was to study maths and sciences. When they left the groups of young boys behind me were soon arguing about who was going to be best at maths from now on and that they were definitely going to university. The schools there were largely from disadvantaged backgrounds so if it just means a few of them were motivated for more than a few days it makes a huge difference.

### Sally Magnusson, broadcaster

For some years, Sally Magnusson, a television news presenter in Scotland and a graduate of the University, has generously assisted with the James Tait Black literary prizes. Established in 1919, the James Tait Black Memorial Prizes are Britain's oldest literary awards, with prizes for works of fiction and biography; a prize for drama was introduced in 2013. Each year, Sally reads the books submitted for consideration and works with staff and students to select the shortlist of the nominees. At an event at the Edinburgh International Book Festival in August, Sally skilfully interviews the academic judges then presents the prizes. She also comes along to support and give her expertise on other occasions and provides an excellent model of how alumni can help their *alma mater*.

### Chrystal Macmillan, scientist, lawyer and campaigner

The enthusiasm and activity by the relatively recent alumni mentioned above carries on a historical tradition of making a global impact. Chrystal Macmillan was the first woman to graduate from the University in science, in 1896. She went on to become a lawyer, and in another 'first' for women, became the first woman to plead before the House of Lords, making the case (in 1908) that female graduates should be allowed the vote. She was one

James Tait Black Awards 2012 – Professor Jonathan Wild, judge of the Biography Prize, with presenter Sally Magnusson

Chrystal Macmillan's contribution is recognised in the naming of this building in George Square, the home of the School of Social and Political Studies

of the organisers of the International Congress of Women in The Hague in 1915, from which a delegation later presented proposals to heads of neutral states to halt the First World War. After the war, she was a delegate at the Paris Peace Conference in 1919. Called to the English Bar in 1924 as one of the first women admitted, she continued an impressive career as what would now be called a human rights lawyer.

## REGENTS

Originally the professors of the University were called regents but this term gradually fell out of use. In 2012 a new category of supporter was approved by the University Court, and the title of 'regent' is in use once more. Regents are people who give significant support to the University – financially, with their expertise or by sharing their networks.

As the University moves forward, the need for fundraising and help in key areas of development is crucial and the input of different people at different times is vital. The appointment of regents gives the University great flexibility in adapting to change and exploiting new areas of endeavour. A clear understanding of the role of each regent, explicitly reflecting the individual's expertise and the ways in which they will support the University, will deliver huge benefits.

## MOTIVATING THE NEXT GENERATION – OUTREACH TO SCHOOLS

To ensure the continuous flow of talented students through the University it is crucial to engage with schools, teachers, parents and pupils. This may involve helping teachers to deliver lessons with up-to-date context or giving access to equipment the school could not afford, assisting with projects or simply helping to inspire pupils about possibilities. Career options are changing fast and pupils, schools and parents need to know about this.

Particularly important is face-to-face interaction between pupils and role models, and the best interactions are often with people pupils can easily relate to. Current and recent students are well-placed to do this, empathising readily with the choices school students are having to make. In addition to benefiting schools, outreach events give opportunities for University students to share their learning and develop their communication skills. Special attention is given to schools in disadvantaged areas to help raise aspirations.

Some of these outreach activities would not have been possible without philanthropic support. The Sutton Trust is one such example, initially funding the University's 'Pathways to the Professions' project. This very successful activity brings young people from disadvantaged backgrounds into the professions, a career choice many might not have thought open to them. The success of the project depends upon the time and commitment of the University's partners in this enterprise – the professional bodies, such as the Law Society and Royal College of Surgeons, the state schools, families of pupils and, of course, University staff – and has benefited too from support from the Brightside Trust and the Esmée Fairbairn Foundation.

### STUDENTS 'GIVING BACK'

Students too 'give back' to their University, and some of the ways in which they do so have been explored in the chapter on student life. But they also give in other ways not recognised there – such as assisting with Open Day events, working as volunteer guides showing potential students and visitors around the University, acting as class representatives for their peers, serving on committees and arranging hospitality events in halls of residence. Giving in this way helps students develop a number of skills, but also gives them a sense of connection to the University beyond the academic. As one of the graduate interns who conducted some of the research for this book has put it: 'I learned a lot from the research, and in an entirely non-academic and sentimental way I feel more connected to the University as an institution'.

Students volunteer for many events, including Open Days

Our volunteering centre links students with the community while they are studying at the University; some of their activities are mentioned in the chapters on student life and scholarships. Students work in close partnership with organisations across the city. Over 2,000 students gave time last year to volunteer on diverse projects including: providing company for old people; helping vets treat pets; providing help with dementia care, children's hospices and social enterprises; giving children's parties; cleaning up playgrounds and beaches; and painting an emergency hostel for homeless people. The students benefit enormously as do those receiving their help, and we hope it develops in them an awareness of the importance of giving their time and using their skills to help others.

## LEARNING IN THE COMMUNITY –
## THE INPUT OF STUDENTS AND STAFF

With a combination of student volunteering and voluntary input from members of the legal profession and University staff, the Free Legal Advice Centre is run by law students for the benefit of people living in and around Edinburgh. The students participating in the Centre are graduate lawyers completing either the Diploma in Legal Practice or a Masters programme. Students are supervised by qualified solicitors and give advice on a wide range of problems including family law issues, debt management, and landlord and tenant disputes.

New in 2013–14 is a partnership working course aimed at students on professionally qualifying programmes such as law, social work, architecture, education and psychology. Students work in multi-agency teams to provide a 'service design' and a 'built design' solution to a current public policy problem. Students are expected to scope and research the policy problem (no reading lists!) and think creatively about solutions. As part of the course the student teams will develop and run a community engagement session aimed at raising public awareness of the issues underlying the policy problem and gaining feedback on solutions proposed. Throughout the course students will be given core skills training on leadership; team working and negotiation; ethics, confidentiality and data sharing; and effective presentation techniques. Again, this is a wonderful example of how staff can develop the culture of philanthropy in the next generation.

## ALUMNI SUPPORTING THE FUTURE

Alumni support their *alma mater* in numerous ways, and an excellent example of how a group of alumni can help the University collectively as well as individually is demonstrated by the Alumni Club in Toronto. The Edinburgh University Club of Toronto (EDUCT) set up a Geography Centenary Fund. The endowment of approximately £35,000 they raised through this is being used to support small scholarships for students and for a lecture in the name of James Wreford Watson (1936 BA) who was a Scottish/Canadian geographer and cartographer. They are now leading a campaign to raise £50,000 for a Decennial Fund to celebrate the tenth anniversary of EDUCT in support of the University.

CONTRIBUTIONS FROM STAFF

A final word on gifts in kind must recognise the enormous contributions made by the staff of the University. Yes, of course, staff are paid to do a job, but so many staff see their work at the University as much more than a job, and they too provide support both at the University and in the wider community. Beyond the University, academic staff serve on review and grant panels to award funding for research and ensure standards for publication. Staff give seminars internationally and help develop policy with research councils and governments, and many give their time to help and support educational institutions across the developing world.

The professors commissioned this portrait of Principal Robertson in 1793 from Henry Raeburn

In 1792, the newly formed Symposium Academicum, a 'social convention' of professors designed to meet annually for a dinner and discussion, decided to commission Henry Raeburn to paint a portrait of Principal Robertson, the cost of which would be shared amongst the twenty-seven professors. The portrait was completed shortly before Robertson's death in 1793. In 1798, the Symposium decided to commission another portrait from Raeburn, this time of Lord Provost Elder, in recognition of his 'indefatigable exertions in bringing and advancing the new buildings for the College of Edinburgh'. Raeburn's portraits of Robertson and Elder are among many fine portraits on display in Old College, the 'new buildings' referred to in the Symposium's appreciation of Elder.

The current focus of staff contributions may have changed since the eighteenth century, but the tradition of giving continues in many ways. Hearing the concern expressed by a catering assistant who has noticed that a new student is not eating much, watching a servitor patiently giving directions to a lost tourist or seeing the outreach programmes run with local schools, it is clear that staff contribute in a vast range of ways beyond merely doing their job, often giving up evenings and weekends for field trips, seminars and workshops. In addition to these informal contributions to the University and the city, staff volunteer for a range of roles, such as hosting international students in their own homes, assisting with events in the Chaplaincy, providing time and expertise to local charities or working with children's panels, political parties or councils. Others help students organise events that provide support, like the *pro bono* work of the Law School.

Staff support each other as well as the institution, mentoring colleagues in other areas of the University or volunteering as representatives in the recognised trade unions. In this latter role, in addition to supporting individual colleagues, staff have a significant input to governance by working in partnership with Human Resources and managers to develop and improve the University's staffing policies.

Sophia Jex-Blake campaigned energetically for the right of women to be admitted to the University in the 1860s, specifically to study medicine. That she succeeded in having women permitted to matriculate and attend classes in 1869 was largely due to the support of several members of staff. Of course, there were opponents to the cause. One notable example was Professor Robert Christison, though

he gave much support to the University in other ways, in particular to the development of sporting facilities. In a complex and lengthy legal battle, the decision to allow women to matriculate was reversed, and it was to be some years before women were formally admitted to the University. Crucial to their campaign was the work of Professor David Masson, as noted in Chapter 8, and the time and energy devoted by Masson and his colleagues can only be imagined.

Staff today continue these traditions of helping the University as a community, with a culture of philanthropy embedded in the University and in the higher education sector in general.

# 10

# Motivations for Giving, and Looking to the Future

MOTIVATIONS

**P**EOPLE SUPPORT FINE CAUSES for many different reasons. Some benefactions are made in gratitude for a service rendered, others are made in the hope of future improvements which will alleviate suffering experienced by a donor or their family, and some gifts are made as a way of ensuring a collection continues to stay together to benefit future generations. The distinction of University Benefactor was established in 2005 to recognise individuals and organisations that have made a significant contribution to the University.

The Polish School of Medicine Memorial Fund is an example of philanthropy in gratitude for services rendered. The Fund was set up in 1986 by graduates and friends of the Polish School to acknowledge the help the University had given to Poles during the Second World War and to foster the links between the University of Edinburgh and Polish medical universities. Income from the fund still provides scholarships for talented medical scientists from Polish medical universities to come to Edinburgh to undertake further study or research.

Several of the University's scholarships and bursaries were established by alumni who had been supported financially through their own studies, and the need to increase such funding continues to be a major strategic priority for the University in widening access to students from all backgrounds. For that reason, profits from this book will be channelled into University bursaries.

The collections which have been given to the University over the years continue to be used by staff and students for study and research purposes, but also open the University to the public in ways which improve our links with the city and beyond. The annual Doors Open Day weekend, when many buildings across the city are open to the public, sees several University collections receiving large numbers of visitors – to view the geological and fine art collections, the Anatomy Museum, the Sculpture Court in Edinburgh College of Art and the extensive collections of musical instruments. Of course, visitors also view and appreciate much of the built environment – Old College, the McEwan Hall, St Cecilia's Hall and other fine buildings – many of which were funded wholly or in part through charitable giving.

## LOOKING TO THE FUTURE

This book has, we hope, shown how crucial to the development, success and international influence of the University philanthropy has been over the last 440 years. So what might the future look like? As a University, we seek continuous improvement in the educational experience available to students – to enable our graduates to be leaders across the globe and to ensure that our cutting-edge research has real value and impact for society. We are going to have to continue to raise funds from a variety of sources at a significantly faster rate than previously if we are to realise our ambitions.

We will have to be better at conveying to the wider world the continued value of academic institutions in today's society, despite the political, social and environmental uncertainty all around us. We need to understand why people donate money and goods. We hope this snapshot of the kind of projects supported in the past, the way they have built the University and the impact the University has made through these gifts will, in turn, encourage more people to give. Individuals, charities and foundations support things that are important to them, based on their social and cultural background and life experiences. Through this book, we hope we have evidenced that we will curate gifts with care and deliver what our donors hoped for. Of course our alumni are important, but so are others who wish to ensure that our skills are used to deal with issues of concern, such as treating disease, alleviating poverty, addressing the growing shortage of resources such as oil, gas and key minerals, and coping with the feeding and welfare of a growing world population despite climate change and increased frequency of environmental catastrophes. Working in partnerships with others, the University of Edinburgh can help deliver this by our academic endeavours and the contributions of those who come to us to learn.

With continuous and increased philanthropy we commit to continue to deliver amazing outcomes across a wide range of academic, social, technical, cultural and professional disciplines.

Old College dome at sunset

# About the Authors

JEAN GRIER is Investigations Manager and Research and Projects Officer for the Vice Principals at the University of Edinburgh and was delighted to be asked by Mary Bownes to support this project. Having worked in a variety of interesting posts at the University over the past thirty years, Jean already had a broad knowledge of the scope of the University, but this has been deepened and stimulated considerably by liaising with colleagues across the institution in the writing and illustration of this book. With a background in English Language and Literature, Jean has extensive experience in publishing policy documents, and designs and delivers professional development courses.

MARY BOWNES is a professor of developmental biology and Senior Vice Principal at the University of Edinburgh. After running a successful research team, teaching biology and heading the Institute of Cell and Molecular Biology, Mary became a Vice Principal in 2003, leading strategic development for a broad portfolio of activities. She focused more on engaging with the wider public and became Vice Principal External Engagement when she added Development and Alumni Engagement to her portfolio in 2011. This stimulated her interest in how philanthropy has significantly helped develop and shape the University since its inception in 1583.

# Bibliography

Anderson, R. D., Lynch, M. and Phillipson, N. (2003), *The University of Edinburgh: An Illustrated History*, Edinburgh: Edinburgh University Press.

Burnett, J. H., Howarth, D. and Fletcher, S. D. (1986), *The University Portraits: Second Series*, Edinburgh: University of Edinburgh.

Charnock Bradley, O. (1923), *History of the Edinburgh Veterinary College*, Edinburgh: Oliver and Boyd.

Craufurd, T. (1808), *History of the University of Edinburgh from 1580 to 1646*, Edinburgh: n.p.

Cronshaw, A. (1989), *Edinburgh from Old Picture Postcards*, Edinburgh: Mainstream Publishing Co. (Edinburgh) Ltd.

Donaldson, G. (ed.) (1983), *Four Centuries: Edinburgh University Life 1583–1983*, Edinburgh: Edinburgh University Press.

Edinburgh University Union and Catto, I. (1989), '*No Spirits and Precious Few Women': Edinburgh University Union 1889–1989*, Edinburgh: Edinburgh University Union.

Finlayson, C. P. (1958), 'Illustrations of games by a seventeenth century Edinburgh student', *The Scottish Historical Review* 37, 1–10.

Fraser, A. G. (1989), *The Building of Old College*, Edinburgh: Edinburgh University Press.

Grant, A. (1884), *The Story of the University of Edinburgh*, London: Longmans, Green and Co.

Gray, J. G. (1977), *Prophet in Plimsoles: An Account of the Life of Colonel Ronald B. Campbell*, Edinburgh: n.p.

Guthrie, D. (1964), *The Medical School of Edinburgh*, Edinburgh: University of Edinburgh.

Higgins, P. (2002), 'Outdoor education in Scotland', *Journal of Adventure Education and Outdoor Learning* 2, 149–68.

Horn, D. B. (1967), *A Short History of the University of Edinburgh 1556–1889*, Edinburgh: Edinburgh University Press.

Knox, H. M. (1953), *Two Hundred and Fifty Years of Scottish Education 1696–1946*, Edinburgh: Oliver and Boyd.

Knox, J., 'The necessity of schools', in H. Craik (ed.) (1916), *English Prose*, New York: The Macmillan Company.

Logan Turner, A. (1933), *History of the University of Edinburgh 1883–1933*, London: Oliver and Boyd.

*The McEwan Hall* (1897), special edition of *The Student: Edinburgh University Magazine*.

Munro, R. (1882), *Ancient Scottish Lake-Dwellings or Crannogs*, Edinburgh: David Douglas.

*The New Amphion: Being the Book of the Edinburgh University Fancy Fair* (1886), Edinburgh: David Douglas.

Rostowski, J. (1955), *History of the Polish School of Medicine: University of Edinburgh*, Edinburgh: University of Edinburgh.

Stewart, C. H. (1973), *The Past Hundred Years: The Buildings of the University of Edinburgh*, Edinburgh: Edinburgh University Press.

Talbot Rice, D. (1957), *The University Portraits*, Edinburgh: Edinburgh University Press.

Tomaszewski, W. (1968), *The University of Edinburgh and Poland: An Historical Review*, Edinburgh: Tomaszewksi.

Turnbull, M. (1987), *Edinburgh Portraits*, Edinburgh: John Donald.

*University of Edinburgh: Three Hundred and Fiftieth Anniversary 1583–1933: Records of the Celebration* (1933), Edinburgh: Oliver and Boyd (reprinted from the *Commemoration Number of the University Journal*).

Usher, C. M. (ed.) (1966), *The Story of Edinburgh University Athletic Club*, Edinburgh: n.p.

Watt, H., Hunter, A. M. and Curtis, W. A. (1946), *New College Edinburgh: A Centenary History*, Edinburgh: Oliver and Boyd.

Wintersgill, D. (2005), *The Rectors of the University of Edinburgh 1859–2000*, Edinburgh: Dunedin Academic Press.

Youngson, A. J. (1966), *The Making of Classical Edinburgh*, Edinburgh: Edinburgh University Press.

# Acknowledgements

A book of this type obviously owes its existence to many people. It has been very much a collaborative effort and, almost without fail, those to whom requests for information were made have responded promptly and enthusiastically. Indeed, one of the frustrations of producing this book has been how to keep the project within manageable bounds! Each one of the topics covered by a chapter could have become a book in its own right – hundreds of bursaries and scholarship funds, dozens of funded chairs, art works and library gifts which there hasn't been space to mention, and each of them with a story to tell about why the gift came to the University and how it has contributed to the University's development.

Particular thanks must go to the postgraduate students who researched material for chapters – Rebecca van Hove, Siobhan Magee, Thomas Farrington and St John Grier – and the staff they worked with, especially Jim Aitken, Hazel Blair and Robert Lawrie. From the outset, we knew that illustrations were going to be key to the success of this book, and staff in the Centre for Research Collections – Grant Buttars, Jill Forrest, Rachel Hosker, Joe Marshall, Neil Lebeter and colleagues – provided a great deal of guidance and support, working with postgraduate student Thibaut Clamart who carried out much of the picture research. Katja Robinson worked with Thibaut on some of the illustrations and was invaluable in checking permissions, pulling the picture credits together and preparing materials for the publishers – a complex task in a fully illustrated book. Barbara Laing and Susan Halcro in Communications and Marketing provided guidance on photographic illustrations and design, and Niall Bradley advised on marketing.

The seminal work on the history of the University is the volume written by R. D. Anderson, M. Lynch and N. Phillipson in 2003 when they were all members of staff at the University. Michael Lynch was very understanding of our attempt to canter through Scotland's history in a few pages, and was indulgent of shameless plagiarism and attempts to précis *The University of Edinburgh: An Illustrated History*.

Similarly, Andrew G. Fraser, who wrote the definitive *The Building of Old College* in 1989, very generously contributed a summary of his own work for this volume. Ian Catto edited a volume in 1989 celebrating 100 years of Edinburgh University Union, and kindly allowed the reprinting of a substantial quotation from that work.

Historical information was sourced from many other older works, which are listed in the bibliography. More recent information was largely supplied by current members of staff, and has involved colleagues from across the University. Estates and Buildings, staff in Information Services and especially in the Centre for Research Collections, colleagues in the Scholarship and Student Funding Office, in Development and Alumni and in the Centre for Sport and Exercise all helped, as did staff in EUSA and in many academic departments and Schools.

On the production side, Angela Penman very patiently disentangled multiple drafts of the text as they travelled through the ether between Jean and Mary, and staff at Edinburgh University Press, in particular Ian Davidson and Edward Clark, guided the book through the production stages, with meticulous copy-editing by Anna Stevenson. Simon Miles and Alan Brown reviewed proposals for the book at an early stage and made many helpful suggestions. Andrew Fraser kindly read and commented on the full manuscript before it went to press and, with his wealth of knowledge and eye for detail, was particularly helpful in spotting inconsistencies. Any errors remaining are down to the authors.

We have attempted to list contributors and advisers below, but are aware that there will be many others who perhaps looked something up, dug out a dusty file for someone or contributed information subsequently summarised by a Head of School or College. Others sent us large volumes of material which we were able to draw on in writing this book. Our thanks go to all involved, but especially to the donors – past, present and yet to come – without whom this University would not have developed as it has done.

Our thanks go to:

Jim Aitken
Thomas Aquilina
David Argyle
Cliff Barraclough
Hazel Blair
Mark Blaxter
Raj Bhopal
George Boag
Barbara Bompani
Niall Bradley
Chris Breward
Jennifer Brown

Malcolm Brown
Grant Buttars
Ian Catto
Thibaut Clamart
Shuna Colville
Andrew Cronshaw
Angus Currie
Jane Dawson
Rebecca Devon
Maria Dlugolecka-Graham
Thomas Farrington
David Finnegan

Jill Forrest
Paul Foster
Andrew Fraser
Peter Freshwater
St John Grier
Susan Halcro
Claudia Hopkins
Rachel Hosker
Jane Johnston
Chloe Kippen
Barbara Laing
Robert Lawrie
David Leach
Neil Lebeter
Cheryl Loney
Michael Lynch
Lesley McAra
Jacky McBeath

Gillian MacCay
Siobhan Magee
Joe Marshall
Darryl Martin
Scott Murray
Zoe Patterson
Angela Penman
Sarah Purves
Ian Ralston
Lizzie Robertson
Katja Robinson
Pam Smith
John Smyth
Gordon Thomas
Rebecca van Hove
Charles Withers
Lesley Yellowlees

# Illustration Credits

Every effort has been made to trace copyright holders, but if any have been inadvertently overlooked the publisher will be pleased to make the necessary arrangement at the first opportunity.

50 Illustrated London News
   Paul Zanre
51 © The University of Edinburgh
52 Walter Scott Image Collection © The
   University of Edinburgh
   Architectural Drawings © The University
   of Edinburgh
53 Tricia Malley & Ross Gillespie
   CRC Gallimaufry © The University of
   Edinburgh
54 Paul Dodds
   Mary Evans Picture Library
55 University of Edinburgh: People,
   Places & Events © The University of
   Edinburgh
   Douglas Robertson
57 The National Archives, ref. MPF1/366/1
   Mary Bownes
   Mary Bownes
58 Architectural Drawings © The University
   of Edinburgh
   Architectural Drawings © The University
   of Edinburgh
   Architectural Drawings © The University
   of Edinburgh
59 University of Edinburgh: People,
   Places & Events © The University of
   Edinburgh
   University of Edinburgh: People,
   Places & Events © The University of
   Edinburgh
60 Hugh Pastoll
61 University of Edinburgh: People,
   Places & Events © The University of
   Edinburgh
   Paul Dodds
62 University of Edinburgh: People,
   Places & Events © The University of
   Edinburgh
   Architectural Drawings © The University
   of Edinburgh
63 Paul Dodds
64 Architectural Drawings © The University
   of Edinburgh
   Tricia Malley and Ross Gillespie
65 © The University of Edinburgh
66 Douglas Robertson Photography,
   douglasinscotland.co.uk
68 Chris Park
70 University of Edinburgh: People,
   Places & Events © The University of
   Edinburgh
71 University of Edinburgh: People,
   Places & Events © The University of
   Edinburgh
   University of Edinburgh: People,
   Places & Events © The University of
   Edinburgh
   CRC Gallimaufry © The University of
   Edinburgh

72 © The University of Edinburgh
   Paul Dodds
   © The University of Edinburgh
   Paul Dodds
73 © The University of Edinburgh
75 © The University of Edinburgh
76 © The University of Edinburgh
77 Photograph by Professor Albert Simeoni
   – with kind permission from Jean
   Rushbrook
79 Paul Dodds
80 Material provided by D. Richard
   Torrance
   Laing Collection © The University of
   Edinburgh
   Laing Collection © The University of
   Edinburgh
   CRC Gallimaufry © The University of
   Edinburgh
81 Tricia Malley and Ross Gillespie
83 Matt Davis, shashin.co.uk
   Douglas Robertson Photography,
   douglasinscotland.co.uk
84 © The University of Edinburgh
85 David Stirling, TooManyColours.co.uk
   Douglas Robertson Photography,
   douglasinscotland.co.uk
89 Jean Grier
90 CRC Gallimaufry © The University of
   Edinburgh
91 www.fionnacarlisle.com
92 Material provided by Jean Grier
95 © The University of Edinburgh
96 Mary Evans Picture Library
   Cheryl Loney
97 Material provided by University of
   Edinburgh
   National Archives of Australia: A1200,
   L22900
100 Foster + Partners, London, 2013
    Thomas Aquilina
101 Object Lessons © The University of
    Edinburgh
102 © The University of Edinburgh
105 © The University of Edinburgh
108 © The University of Edinburgh
109 © The University of Edinburgh
111 © The University of Edinburgh
    Object Lessons © The University of
    Edinburgh
112 © The University of Edinburgh
    The Scotsman Publications Ltd
    The Scotsman Publications Ltd
    A. Theo Marshall
113 © The University of Edinburgh
115 Image courtesy of Heritage and
    Information Governance, Heriot-Watt
    University
120 © The University of Edinburgh
122 Cheryl Loney

# Index

Note: illustrations are indicated by page numbers in bold